VICTORIA AND ALBERT MUSEUM   LONDON 1972

CATALOGUE OF ADAM PERIOD FURNITURE

MAURICE TOMLIN

Printed in England for Her Majesty's Stationery Office by Curwen Press
Dd 647009 K32 0/72

SBN 901486 442

CONTENTS

ACKNOWLEDGEMENTS

I should like to thank the following for the help and co-operation I have received in the preparation of this book: Mrs Helena Hayward, Mr and Mrs John Harris and my colleagues in the Department of Furniture and Woodwork and at Osterley Park. I am particularly indebted to Sir John Summerson and Miss Dorothy Stroud for allowing me to examine and reproduce many of the Adam drawings at the Soane Museum.

M.F.T.

NOTE

A large amount of furniture from the Victoria and Albert Museum's collection is away on loan to other museums and to houses belonging to the National Trust. As this amounts to well over six hundred items in all, it has not been practicable to include these pieces, which are, as a whole, of secondary importance when compared with the furniture that remains in the Museum and at Osterley Park. It is hoped, however, to include entries for these items in later editions of this catalogue, together with information about subsequent additions to the Museum's collection.

INTRODUCTION

The furniture in this volume, dating from between 1760 and 1800, is either wholly or partly in the Neo-Classical style. Robert Adam, though not the first designer to introduce Neo-Classical features into English furniture, was the leading exponent of the style in this country. His working life, from his return to this country from Italy in 1758 to his death in 1792, coincides almost exactly with the period under review. Commenting on the all-pervading influence of Adam's style on his contemporaries, Sir John Soane, addressing the students of the Royal Academy in 1823, said, 'The light and elegant ornaments, the varied compartments in the ceilings of Mr. Adam, imitated from Ancient Works in the Baths and Villas of the Romans, were soon applied in designs for chairs, tables, carpets and in every other species of furniture. To Mr. Adam's taste in the ornament of his buildings and furniture we stand indebted, inasmuch as manufacturers of every kind felt, as it were, the electric power of this revolution in art.'

The most important group of furniture included in this Catalogue is that designed between 1767 and 1779 by Adam, or under his supervision, for the State Rooms at Osterley Park. This furniture is still at the house, the contents of which come under the jurisdiction of the Victoria and Albert Museum. The first entries in the Catalogue, however, concern several items of furniture which date from the earliest phase of Neo-Classicism in England, made before Adam was engaged on the furnishing of Osterley.

After the Osterley furniture other items with which Adam was directly concerned are discussed; then follows a section devoted to other grand pieces closely related to Adam's work.

The subsequent sections of the Catalogue are mainly devoted to furniture of the kind commonly known as 'Hepplewhite', in which the style used by Adam for his State Rooms has been modified and simplified for a wider market. In many of these pieces the retention of Rococo features can be seen although the decoration is in the Neo-Classical idiom. Furniture of similar character, related to the earlier designs of Sheraton, as illustrated in his *Drawing Book*, has also been included. Items in the manner of Sheraton's later pattern-books—where a distinctly new, early nineteenth-century, character appears—will be discussed in a subsequent volume.

The early manifestations of Neo-Classicism in England have been extensively studied and discussed and new information is continually coming to light. Moreover, a great deal of scholarship has been devoted to works on Adam and his contemporaries. Since this information is readily available elsewhere, no attempt is made here to survey this interesting phase in the history of the decorative arts in England. Introductory sections giving background information are kept quite short in those instances where it is possible to refer the reader to general works on the subject. A select bibliography is included and more specific references may be found under individual catalogue entries.

Maurice Tomlin
London, 1969

BOOKS REFERRED TO IN
ABBREVIATED FORM

Adam
The Works in Architecture. By Robert and James Adam. 2 vols. London, 1773–79; third volume, 1822.

Chippendale
The Gentleman and Cabinet-Maker's Director. By Thomas Chippendale. 1st ed. London, 1754; 2nd ed. 1755; 3rd ed. 1762.

Harris
The Furniture of Robert Adam. By Eileen Harris. London, 1963.

Hepplewhite
The Cabinet-Maker and Upholsterer's Guide. By A. Hepplewhite and Co. 1st ed. London, 1788; 2nd ed. 1789; 3rd ed. 1794.

MacQuoid and Edwards
The Dictionary of English Furniture. By Percy MacQuoid and Ralph Edwards. 2nd ed. London, 1954.

Musgrave
Adam and Hepplewhite and other Neo-Classical Furniture. By Clifford Musgrave. London, 1966.

Russell
Catalogue of Musical Instruments, Victoria and Albert Museum, vol. I, *Keyboard Instruments*. By Raymond Russell. London, 1968.

Sheraton
The Cabinet-Maker and Upholsterer's Drawing Book. By Thomas Sheraton. London, 1791–94.

GROUP A

Early Neo-Classical furniture

This group comprises early essays in Neo-Classicism, in many of which the difficulty of adapting old forms to the new decorative idiom is apparent. For example, the Chippendale chair (A/1), although decorated with Neo-Classical motifs, still retains an Early Georgian shape. In the chair (A/4) the designer has displayed his hesitancy in the awkward distortion of the columnar back legs at their junction with the seat-rail. On the other hand, the pedestal of similar date (A/2) is completely Neo-Classical in both form and decoration.

A/1

A/1 ARMCHAIR

Beech, carved and gilded; covered with a contemporary crimson damask (not original); brass castors.
From a suite of 8 armchairs and 4 sofas.
About 1765.
Height 106.5 cm. (42 in.).
W.1–1937.

This suite of armchairs and sofas is important for being the only furniture known to have been made by Thomas Chippendale to a design by Robert Adam. It was made for 19 Arlington Street, the London house of Sir Laurence Dundas. Adam's design for the sofa, dated 1764, is in the Soane Museum (vol. 17, no. 74; pl. A/1a) and his account to Sir Laurence Dundas for the *Design of Sophas & Chairs for ye Saloone*, dated 18 July 1765, came to £5. Chippendale's account for supplying the furniture, dated 9 July 1765, is as follows: *To 8 large Arm Chairs exceeding Richly Carv'd in the Antick manner & Gilt in oil Gold Stuff'd and cover'd with your own*

Damask and strong Castors on the feet £160
4 large Sofas Exceeding Rich to Match the Chairs £216

This chair was executed from one of Adam's earliest designs for seat furniture and has relief decoration of typical Neo-Classical motifs, including sphinxes and anthemia, applied to what is basically an Early Georgian shape, one that is in strong contrast to his later chair designs (cf. the hall seats at Osterley, B/1, which show a similar Kentian influence, with a tentative use of the straight, fluted leg). However, a fully Neo-Classical design for a *Sopha for Sir Laurence Dundas, Bart.* apparently dates from the same year, 1764 (*Musgrave*, pl. 16).

The motifs carved on the legs of the chairs occur again on the panels of the six pedestals (A/2), which were also designed by Adam for 19 Arlington Street.

(*Harris*, pl. 102, and A. Coleridge, 'Sir Laurence Dundas and Chippendale', *Apollo*, vol. LXXXVI, September 1967.)

A/1a

A/2

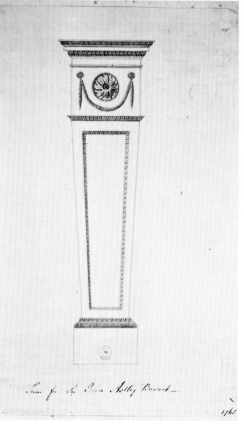

A/2a

A/2   PEDESTAL

Carved pine, painted white and partly gilded.
One of a pair. *En suite* with four similar but
slightly larger pedestals.
About 1765.
Height 137 cm. (54 in.). The larger ones:
Height 146 cm. (57½ in.).
Given by the National Art-Collections Fund.
W.25–1954.

The pedestals were designed by Adam in about
1765 for the same room as the armchairs (A/1)
at 19 Arlington Street. The design no longer
exists but there is an account from Adam,
dated 18 July 1765, containing the entry
Design of Terms for Ditto £3. 3s., which
presumably refers to these pedestals and
follows directly after a reference to *Sophas &
Chairs for ye Saloone.*

There are two very similar designs by Adam,
both dated 1765, the first (Soane Museum, vol.
17, no. 58; pl. A/2a) for Sir John Astley of
Patshull, Staffordshire, and the other (Soane
Museum, vol. 17, no. 59; pl. A/2b) for Sir
John Griffin Griffin. The latter was executed
and is now at Audley End.

This pedestal is the earliest piece of furniture
in the Museum's collection conceived in a fully
Neo-Classical manner. The carving of inter-
twined garlands, surmounted by an anthemion, resembles that on the legs of the armchair, A/1. Since a surviving bill shows that
the chair was supplied by Chippendale, it
seems very likely that he also supplied these
pedestals although they cannot be identified in
the accounts (*Harris*, pl. 131).

A/2b

A/3 CANDELABRUM

Derbyshire fluor-spar (Blue John), mounted
with ormolu, on a base of white marble.
One of a pair.
About 1765.
Height 82.5 cm. (32½ in.).
Given by the National Art-Collections Fund.
W.23–1934.

Made at the Soho (Birmingham) factory of
Matthew Boulton. Like the armchairs (A/1)
and the pedestals (A/2) these candelabra were
formerly at 19 Arlington Street.

The catalogue of Boulton and Fothergill's sale
at Christie and Ansell's in April 1771, includes
the item *A magnificent Persian Candelabra for
7 lights, in which is inserted a vase of the largest
and most beautiful piece of radix amethysti the
mines hath ever produced, which with the double
branches &c. is supported by three Persians,
finely modelled, standing on triangular plynth
of statuary marble ornamented with military
trophies proper for the subject.* (The seventh
light would have been on the underside of the
reversible lid.)

There is in the Assay Office Library at
Birmingham a letter from Boulton and
Fothergill to Sir Laurence Dundas, dated
4 January 1772, reporting the despatch by
wagon of *a large radix amethysti vase
supported by three Persian slaves* and stating
that this had been ordered at the time of the
sale. The conclusion drawn from this is that
Sir Laurence Dundas acquired one candelabrum just after the sale (it had been bought in
for £190 10s. 0d.) at the same time ordering a
second one to be made to the same pattern.

A/4   ARMCHAIR

Gilded wood; the upholstery, modern; brass
castors.
1760/65.
Height 96.5 cm. (38 in.).
W.14–1967.

This chair appears to be an early attempt to
design a piece of seat furniture in the Neo-
Classical style. It has a number of features
which have caused it to be linked with the seat
furniture from the Principal Floor of Spencer
House, London, which was being decorated in
the Neo-Classical style by James 'Athenian'
Stuart between 1758/9 and 1768. The shape of
the back and the quite distinctive catch at the
back (for releasing the padded section when
re-upholstering) are features also found on
three sets of chairs made for Spencer House
between about 1760 and 1765, probably by the
important chairmaker John Gordon, who is
known to have supplied furniture to the
Spencer family. The guilloche motif, which is
in a version much used by Stuart in his
decoration at Spencer House, appears again on
the chairs designed by him for the Painted
Room in 1759. But, in particular, the legs of
this chair are very similar to those on several
pieces of furniture from Lady Spencer's
apartment. The tables and case-furniture for
this room, which are very early examples of
Neo-Classical furniture, executed under
Stuart's guidance, are now in the Spencer
collection at Althorp, Northamptonshire. The
chairs, however, are apparently no longer in
the Spencer collection. The suggestion is,
therefore, put forward that this may be one of
the chairs made for Lady Spencer's bedroom at
Spencer House. (The set designed by Stuart in
1759 for the Painted Room is currently on loan
to the Iveagh Bequest at Kenwood from Lord
Spencer's collection.)

The chair has been re-gilded and the gesso
carving is no longer very sharp.

A/4

A/5   U R N S on P E D E S T A L S (a pair)
Mahogany, with brass mounts; the urns lined
with lead.
About 1765.
Height 162 cm. (63¾ in.).
Given by John A. Talk Esq.
W.38 & a–1934.

The urns are fitted with loop handles, which
have chased brass back-plates in the form of
lion-masks. The taps are in the form of eagles
with outstretched wings.

One pedestal has a cupboard, the lower half of
which contains a drawer on brass rollers with
compartments for four bottles. Below this
there is another drawer, lined with green
baize. The cupboard of the other pedestal
extends down to the plinth and has a single
shelf, the whole of the interior being lined
with green baize. Set into the plinth is a
shallow drawer on rollers, which is also lined
with green baize.

A sideboard table, flanked by a pair of urns on
pedestals, was often used by Adam to form an
important decorative unit in a dining-room.
'Designs for Pedestals' had appeared already
in 1762 in *Chippendale*, 3rd ed. The pedestals
shown here are of similar type, with Neo-
Classical, instead of Rococo, ornament.
Hepplewhite, 1st ed., 1788, illustrates six
examples (pls. 35 and 36) which are more
pronouncedly Neo-Classical, having straight
sides to the pedestals. Later these pedestals
were incorporated in the actual sideboard, as
shown in plate 21 of *Sheraton*. Very often one
of the pedestals was fitted with a metal rack,
so that the plates could be heated by a small oil
burner below.

A/6 PICTURE FRAME
Gilded wood.
About 1766.
Height 241 cm. (95 in.).
W.36–1949.

This is an exceptionally fine example of a picture-frame in the Neo-Classical style. The elaborate cresting incorporates a relief carving of Minerva and Cupid.

The oil painting, signed *Pompeo Battoni* and dated 1766, is of Edward Howard, 2nd son of the Hon. Phillip Howard.

Since John Linnell supplied furniture for another branch of the family at Castle Howard, it is possible that he also made this frame. The surmounting medallion is reminiscent of similar features on other pieces of furniture designed by him (eg the sofa at Kedleston Hall; *Harris*, pl. 98).

A/7 MASTER'S CHAIR
Mahogany, carved and inlaid; upholstered in dark green leather.
About 1760.
Height 178 cm. (70 in.).
W.10–1923.

The heavy proportions and high back are typical characteristics of chairs designed for ceremonial use.

The brass plates on the insides of the front legs were for attaching a foot-rest. The chair originally had castors.

A/7

GROUPS B to M

Osterley Park:
Introduction

The following twelve groups deal with the furniture from Osterley Park, which Adam was engaged in re-modelling between 1761 and 1780.

Although most of the furniture was designed by Adam himself, it is now believed that John Linnell, one of the leading cabinet-makers and designers of the time, not only made a great deal of the furniture but was also responsible for many of the designs. Adam invariably seems to have supplied designs for pieces that were closely integrated with the architecture, such as pier-glasses and side-tables, but in many cases he probably supplied at most only rough sketches for chairs and other more mobile furniture, leaving Linnell to work out the designs in detail.

Many of Adam's designs for Osterley are among the large collection of his drawings at the Soane Museum. There are also some on exhibition at the house, though these are mostly for the architecture, rather than the furniture. Such designs as are known to exist are mentioned under the appropriate item. Unfortunately, few records referring to the furniture have survived and, in fact, Robert Child himself is known to have destroyed those for the State Bedchamber because he did not wish it to be known how much it had cost him. John Linnell's name is linked with Osterley in a few relatively unimportant surviving documents. His father, William, had also had connections with the Child family and after his death in 1763 John took over the business in Berkeley Square, where Robert Child also had his town house. A certain William Linnell, perhaps a son, was also employed, together with Israel Lewis, an upholsterer, to draw up an inventory of the contents of Osterley after the

death of Robert Child in 1782. Most of the Osterley furniture in this book can be identified in this inventory and the entries are included where relevant. In the case of the two lacquer commodes, I/1 and I/2, the suggestion is put forward that they may have been supplied by Chippendale to his own designs, though under the general direction of Adam.

The remarkable feature of Osterley is that the furniture which was actually designed for each of the State Rooms has survived. The furniture for each room is here dealt with as a separate group and is set out in chronological order, as far as this is possible. A few important items that are not part of the original furnishings of the State Rooms have been included but other pieces of minor importance belonging to the house are dealt with in later sections of the catalogue (Q/15, Q/16, Q/17, Q/18, S/6, S/7, S/12, Y/2).

GROUP B

Osterley Park:
Furniture in the Great Hall

The following group of furniture was designed
for the Great Hall at Osterley Park,
Middlesex.

The seats, brackets and lamps can be attributed
to Adam, although no designs for the seats are
known. Adam's designs at the house for the
hall itself are dated 1767 and it is reasonable
to assume that the brackets and lamps were
designed at about the same time, though the
seats are a little more difficult to date. The
pedestals do not appear to have been designed
by Adam and were probably supplied by Sir
William Chambers.

B/1   HALL SEAT
Mahogany and pine, painted white;
upholstered in blue leather (modern).
One of a set of 4.
Height 76 cm. (30 in.).
O.P.H.230–1949.

The inventory of 1782 lists *Four long carved
and painted Scrole end Stools covered with blue
leather*.

There is a rough sketch in the Soane Museum
(vol. 54, no. 66) which has several similar
features. It is for a four-legged seat with
scrolled ends which has a seat-rail decorated
in a manner similar to the Osterley seats. The
legs are heavy, terminating in paw feet, but
the rams' heads are at the level of the seat-rail
and do not form part of the leg. There is no
inscription or date on the sketch.

These seats apparently show Adam still
searching for an appropriate design for seat-
furniture in the Neo-Classical style and still
show strong Kentian influence, particularly in
the corner legs, with their heavy naturalistic
paw feet. The lighter intermediate legs show
the introduction of the columnar, Neo-Classical

B/1

form but even here the paw foot is retained.

It is surprising to find such a tentative essay in Neo-Classicism at such a late date—for the Hall was designed in 1767. Adam's design for a *Sopha for Sir Laurence Dundas, Bart.* (Soane Museum, vol. 17, no. 73), apparently dating from 1764, already has straight legs and is of an entirely Neo-Classical form (*Musgrave*, pl. 16). On the other hand, Adam's other design for a sofa for the same client (Soane Museum, vol. 17, no. 74), which is *en suite* with the armchair in this Museum (A/1), and also dated 1764, is of Early Georgian form even though some of

the details are of Neo-Classical type. (The paws on the central legs of the seats, with their collars, are in fact very reminiscent of the latter design.) Possibly an earlier or rejected design was used when the Osterley Hall came to be furnished.

H. Avray Tipping, 'Osterley Park, II', *Country Life*, 27 November 1926, p. 825, says that 'the faded blue leather with which they are upholstered was put on by Mrs. Child eight years after her husband's death' (ie in 1790) but the blue leather mentioned in the 1782 inventory was presumably the original covering.

B/2

B/2   LAMP
Gilded wood.
One of a pair.
Height 33 cm. (13 in.).
O.P.H.202–1949.

The inventory of 1782 lists *Carved vases and branches to carry three lights each*, intended to stand on a pair of brackets (B/3).

The sketch for the lamps (Soane Museum, vol. 6, no. 33) inscribed *Hall at Osterley, Robt Child Esqr.*, also shows bracket B/3.

B/3

B/3   BRACKET
Pine, carved and painted white.
One of a pair.
Height 38 cm. (15 in.).
O.P.H.200–1949.

The inventory of 1782 lists *Two carved and painted bracketts with carved vases and branches to carry three lights each*.

Designed to support the lamp O.P.H.202–1949 (B/2). Like the hall seats, these show the lingering influence of William Kent, the inspiration possibly coming from a design by Kent for a table for Chiswick House, which was itself based on a Corinthian capital (J. Vardy, *Some designs of Mr. Inigo Jones and Mr. William Kent*, London, 1744, pl. 40).

B/4

B/4   PEDESTAL

Pine, painted white.
One of a set of 4.
Height 106.5 cm. (42 in.).
O.P.H.212–1949.

The inventory of 1782 lists *Four elegant Marble Vases with Basic Relieve figures on carved and painted Pedestals.*

The rather heavy design of these pedestals suggests the hand of Sir William Chambers rather than that of Adam. Chambers was already engaged on re-modelling Osterley before Adam appeared on the scene and the vases and pedestals may well have been supplied by him for the Hall and retained by Adam when he took over.

There is a bill from John Gilbert, dated May 1774, for *No. 2 Pedistalls to Hall at Osterly Inriched with Oak Leaves and Rafled Leaves & c. No. 6 Sides at £2. 18. 6d Each Side £17. 11. 0d.* This is believed to refer to two more, slightly smaller pedestals, carved on only three sides but otherwise made to the same design, that were formerly at the house and retained by the family. John Gilbert was the carver who made the pine cone finials for the turrets at the corners of the house. (*Chambers's Twentieth Century Dictionary* defines 'raffled' as 'having the edge finely notched' and there are other instances of its use in the eighteenth century in reference to the lobes of acanthus leaves.)

GROUP C

The following group of furniture was designed by Robert Adam for the Eating Room at Osterley Park, Middlesex.

A bill for furniture made by John Linnell for Shardeloes includes *2 Mahogany elbow chairs with harp backs* and mentions two urns *like Mr. Child's*. (Extract from a bill for furniture made by Linnell for William Drake in 1767. R. Edwards and M. Jourdain, *Georgian cabinet makers*, 2nd ed., 1946, p. 53. Robert Child was the owner of Osterley at this time.) It is dated 1767. The only dated designs for furniture for the Eating Room at Osterley are also from that year. It therefore seems reasonable to assume that all the furniture for this room was designed in 1767. It also seems likely that it was all made by John Linnell.

The furniture designed for the room did not include a dining table, although one was added to the furnishings in about 1800. According to the inventory of 1782, three mahogany dining tables stood in the North Passage outside; these Early Georgian gate-leg tables, which still exist, would have been brought into the Eating Room at mealtimes. At other times the chairs would have been formally arranged round the walls, leaving the centre of the room clear.

C/1 CHAIR

Mahogany; the seat upholstered with crimson
leather (now faded to brown) and edged with
a gilded metal bead. One of a set of 12. *En suite*
with 2 armchairs (C/2).
Height 100 cm. (39¼ in.).
O.P.H.171–1949.

The inventory of 1782 lists *Twelve carved Lyre
back Chairs of Mahogany covered with crimson
Morrocco Leather.*

The design for these chairs is in the Soane
Museum (vol. 17, no. 93; pl. C/1a), and is
inscribed *Chair for Robert Child Esqr.* It is
undated.

Dining room chairs were usually made of
mahogany and fitted with leather seats. Since
the chairs were normally arranged round the
walls in a formal manner, the backs would not
be seen, so they are not carved and the metal
bead does not continue round at the back. The
splats are made of 3-ply mahogany. It is
interesting to note that the design of the legs
is echoed in those of the fire-grate.

Of his visit to Osterley in 1773, Horace
Walpole in one of his letters said, 'the chairs
are taken from antique lyres, and make
charming harmony'. (*The letters of Horace
Walpole, Earl of Orford; including numerous
letters now first published from the original
manuscripts, 1735–1797*, ed. Mrs Toynbee,
Oxford, 1903–5.)

C/1a

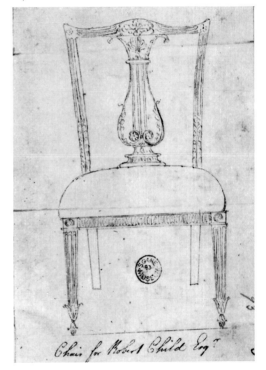

Chair for Robert Child Esqr

C/2 ARMCHAIR

Mahogany; the seat and back upholstered with crimson leather (now faded to brown) and edged with a gilded metal bead.
One of a pair. *En suite* with the 12 side chairs (C/1).
Height 100 cm. (39¼ in.).
O.P.H.183–1949.

The inventory of 1782 lists *Two french Elbow Chairs to match.*

C/3 URN on a PEDESTAL

Mahogany, pine and oak, painted white and partly gilded; ormolu mounts; lead lining to the urn.
One of a pair.
Height 152.5 cm. (60 in.).
O.P.H.185–1949.

The inventory of 1782 lists *Two very elegant Pedestals and vases carved and Japanned White and Gold.*

A bill for furniture made by John Linnell for Shardeloes, Buckinghamshire, dated 1767 (*op. cit.*), states *To making and carving two coopers, the tops in the form of vases and large brass handles like Mr. Child's, and lined with lead to hold water, and the other top a sham.* The Mr Child referred to must have been Robert Child of Osterley. As with the Shardeloes urns, one of the Osterley pair is a 'sham', in that it has a false tap. The Osterley pair is also illustrated in *Adam*, vol. III, 1822, pl. VIII, together with other pieces from Osterley, where they are wrongly described as being 'Furniture at Sion-house'.

C/3

C/4

C/4a

C/4 SIDEBOARD

Gilded pine, with a top of polished mahogany.
Height 86 cm. (33¾ in.).
O.P.H.187–1949.

The inventory of 1782 lists *A Mahogany Sideboard on a carved and very elegant gilt frame.*

The design for this sideboard, on show at Osterley Park, is inscribed *Design of a Table Frame for the Side Board in the Eating Room at Osterly for Robert Child Esqr.* and is dated 1767. In this design the edge of the top is coloured pale green behind the guilloche moulding, whereas in the actual sideboard it is of plain mahogany. There is also an uncoloured sketch in the Soane Museum (vol. 17, no. 7; pl. C/4a), similarly dated 1767. The table is illustrated in *Adam*, vol. III, 1822, pl. VIII, together with other pieces from Osterley, where it is wrongly described as 'Furniture at Sion-house'.

The mahogany top was presumably chosen to harmonize with the other mahogany furniture. (The present high polish cannot be original as the technique of French polishing was not discovered until the early nineteenth century.) Adam favoured the use of the baluster leg on side-tables at this period of his career.

C/5 SIDE-TABLE

Gilded pine, with a top of marble mosaic.
One of a pair.
Height 80.5 cm. (31¾ in.).
O.P.H.188–1949.

The inventory of 1782 lists *Two Antique Mosaic Marble Slabs very highly finished on elegant carved and gilt in burnish Gold Frames with leather covers.* (The leather covers have not survived.)

The design of these tables is very similar to that of the sideboard (C/4), except for the marble mosaic tops, which were probably imported from Italy.

C/5

C/6

C/6　PIER-GLASS
Gilded pine.
One of a pair.
Height 373 cm. (147 in.).
O.P.H.165–1949.

The inventory of 1782 lists *Two large oval pier Glasses in Rich Carved frames with ornaments gilt in burnish Gold plates fifty-six Inches by thirty seven.*

The design for these pier-glasses, which is in the Soane Museum (vol. 20, no. 33; pl. C/6a), is inscribed *For the Eating room at Osterly* and dated 1767.

C/6a

GROUP D

Osterley Park:
Furniture in the Gallery

The following group of furniture was designed
for the Gallery at Osterley Park, Middlesex.
There is a design by Adam, dated 1768, for the
pier-glasses (D/1), and one, dated 1770, for the
girandoles (D/2). It seems likely that the seat
furniture was designed at about the same time
but no designs exist. It is possible that John
Linnell was the maker of the complete set of
furniture for this room.

D/1   PIER-GLASS
Frame of carved and gilded pine.
One of a set of 4.
Height 348 cm. (137 in.).
O.P.H.108–1949.

The inventory of 1782 lists *Four large Pier
Glasses in Elegant carved & Glass bordered
frames rich ornaments at top and bottom the
Plates seventy nine by forty Inches.*

The glasses were designed for four of the ten
piers between the windows, being hung so as
to alternate with the six girandoles (D/2, etc.)
There is a design at the Soane Museum (vol.
20, no. 23, Box 1), inscribed *for the Earl of
Shelburne* and dated 1768, which is identical to
that of these mirrors except that it has festoons
at the base. It also bears a faint pencil
inscription *Glass frame. . . . for Osterly.*

D/2 GIRANDOLE

Frame of carved and gilded pine, with brass candle branches.
One of a set of 6.
Height 228.6 cm. (90 in.).
O.P.H.102–1949.

The inventory of 1782 lists *Six large Elegant Carved and gilt girandoles with plate Glass compartments and four wrought brass branches gilt to each*.

These girandoles were designed for six of the ten piers between the windows, being hung so as to alternate with the four pier-glasses (D/1, etc.). They are based, with slight modifications, on Adam's designs in the Soane Museum (vol. 20, nos. 36 and 37; pls. D/2a and D/2b), inscribed *Girandol for Robert Child Esqr.* and dated 1770. The appearance of the carving suggests that they were made by John Linnell. There are also several designs by Linnell showing similar features (H. Hayward, 'The Drawings of John Linnell in the Victoria and Albert Museum', *Furniture History*, vol. v, 1969, figs. 28, 29, 68).

Note the large size, showing that at this date girandoles were not necessarily small and might well be confused with pier-glasses. The distinction lay in the fact that a girandole had candle branches attached.

D/2a

D/2b

D/5

D/3 ARMCHAIR

Mahogany, partly gilded; the upholstery, modern.
One of a set of 12. *En suite* with 6 settees (see D/4 and D/5).
Height 105.5 cm. (41½ in.).
O.P.H.135–1949.

The inventory of 1782 lists *Twelve large Mahogany french Elbow Chairs to match* (see D/4 and D/5).

No design appears to exist for these chairs but there are points of similarity between these and the chairs designed by Adam for the Eating Room; in particular, the gilded wooden bead round the top of the seat-rail resembles that, executed in gilded metal, on the Eating Room set. There is also a resemblance to some of Adam's designs for settees in the Soane Museum, such as an uninscribed design in vol. 17 (no. 102). The heaviness of the design, not a typical feature of Adam's work, may have been adopted in order to harmonize with the heavier architectural details of the room, which had been designed by Sir William Chambers; it is, at any rate, appropriate for a room of such large proportions. The motif of bound laurels on the seat-rail has been made to echo the moulding of the dado.

D/4 SETTEE

Mahogany, partly gilded; the upholstery modern.
One of a set of 4. *En suite* with 12 armchairs and 2 larger settees (see D/3 and D/5).
Height 103 cm. (40½ in.).
O.P.H.147–1949.

The inventory of 1782 lists *Six large carved Mahogany Soffas covered with pea green Silk and Stuff Damask twelve bolsters and Ten back cushions all in Check Cases.* (These include the two larger settees; see D/5.)

As with the armchairs for this room, although no design is known to exist, they were probably designed by Adam.

On the other hand, as Mrs Hayward points out (H. Hayward, 'The Drawings of John Linnell in the Victoria and Albert Museum', *Furniture History*, vol. v, 1969, fig. 15), the small finial of inverted lotus leaves capping the central front legs was used by Linnell on the backs of the hall settees he designed and made for William Drake. A similar feature appears on the front legs of the Osterley Tapestry Room chairs (G/1).

D/4

D/5   SETTEE

Mahogany, partly gilded; upholstered in late
nineteenth-century crewel-work.
One of a pair. *En suite* with 4 shorter settees
and 12 armchairs (see D/3 and D/4).
Height 109 cm. (43 in.).
O.P.H.151–1949.

For the 1782 inventory entry, see above, under
D/4.

The design of this settee is similar to that of
the smaller type, with a slightly different
treatment of the arms. The upholstery, which
is in the style of the first half of the eighteenth
century, bears the embroidered inscription
A. Z. Fraser, Fecit. 1899.

D/5

GROUP E

Osterley Park:
Furniture in the Library

The following group of furniture, consisting of
8 armchairs, 2 tables and a pedestal desk,
was designed for the Library at Osterley
Park, Middlesex.

Although it is in the Neo-Classical style and the
chairs are furnished with such well-known
Adam motifs as the lyre-back, the design is not
characteristic of the work of Robert Adam.
However, the chair-backs are similar to certain
designs by John Linnell and comparison with
other furniture thought to have been made by
him suggests that this furniture was also both
designed and made by Linnell. French
influence can be seen in this suite, particularly
in the use of ormolu mounts. It dates from
about 1775.

Musgrave, p. 121, draws attention to the
flattening given to the curves of the Vitruvian
scroll where the two directions of the wave-
pattern join in the centre, on both the tables
and the chairs. This characteristic, seen in a
number of Linnell's designs, appears at first
sight to be further welcome evidence
supporting the attribution to Linnell. It is only
fair to note, however, that this is a common
feature of such decoration and can, in fact, be
seen in the Vitruvian scroll of the marble
chimney-piece in the Library, which was
designed by Adam.

E/1a

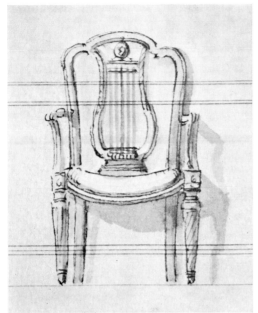

E/1 ARMCHAIR

Mahogany, veneered with rosewood, satinwood
and other woods, some stained green; some
painted decoration; cane seat; ormolu mounts.
One of a set of 8.
Height 89.5 cm. (35¼ in.).
O.P.H.266–1949.

The inventory of 1782 lists *Eight Curious
inlaid Elbow Chairs with Or Molee Ornaments
cane seats Cushions covered with green Leather
and Serge Cases.*

Several of Linnell's designs in the Department
of Prints and Drawings incorporate a lyre-back
with a portrait medallion and one of these
(E.336–1929; pl. E/1a), a design for a room,
shows an armchair with a back very similar to
those of these chairs. The portrait medallion,
of a Classical female head, which is different on
each chair in the set, may be compared with
the cameo heads in the friezes of the Drawing
Room commodes at Osterley and also with the
medallions on the sofas at Kedleston Hall,
Derbyshire, which are the work of Linnell
(*Harris*, p. 89). The panel at the base of the
lyre is of green stained wood with red painted
decoration.

The design of the legs, with their ormolu
swags of very French appearance, is similar to
that of the legs of the steel grates in this room,
which were designed by Adam, and these legs
were presumably modified from Linnell's
original design so as to conform. The upright
acanthus leaf, a motif frequently used by
Linnell, and here seen at the base of the arm
supports, appears again in the library desk
(E/3).

There is at Mersham-le-Hatch, Kent, an
armchair having a rather similar back and a
straight seat-rail, which may be part of the set
supplied by Chippendale in 1767 for the
Dining Parlour there.

E/2 LIBRARY TABLE
Oak and pine, veneered with rosewood,
satinwood and other woods; ormolu mounts;
green baize top.
One of a pair. *En suite* with the library desk
(E/3) and the 8 armchairs (E/1).
Height 77.5cm. (30½in.).
O.P.H.264–1949.

The inventory of 1782 lists *A pair of Library
Tables with three Draws each curiously inlaid
and finished with Or Molee Ornaments lined
with green Cloth*.

There is an almost identical library table at
Alnwick Castle, Northumberland, differing
from the Osterley pair in the form of its feet
and in the treatment of the Vitruvian scroll in
the frieze (no published illustration of this is
known but a related billiard table, also at
Alnwick, is illustrated in *MacQuoid and
Edwards*, vol. III, p. 190, fig. 4). William Linnell
is known to have been employed by the Duke
of Northumberland and, on his death, his son,
John Linnell, took over the firm. Furthermore,

at the time of his death in 1763, William
Linnell was also owed money by Robert
Child, presumably for work at Child's town
house in Berkeley Square. These links with
both the Duke of Northumberland and Robert
Child suggest that Linnell could well have
been the maker of the library tables at both
places. There are several other rather similar
tables, including one made for Temple
Newsam, Leeds, where Linnell is known to
have worked, which has a frieze decorated with
a Greek key-pattern. There is a design by
Adam dated 1765, for a 'table frame' for Sir
Giles Farnaby (Soane Museum, vol. 17, no. 6,
illustrated in *Harris*, pl. 7), which has swags
at the tops of the legs and a Vitruvian scroll
frieze but the other elements of the design
show a lightness and delicacy typical of Adam's
work but not seen in the Osterley tables. This
could have provided the inspiration for their
design, however, although the origin of these
motifs is probably J.-F. de Neufforge's *Recueil
d'Architecture*, which had been published in
nine volumes between 1757 and 1768. French

E/2

tables with similar swags are known but their exact date is uncertain. Such a French table might, however, have provided a model for the design of the Osterley pair. Several designs by Linnell in the Department of Prints and Drawings (E.259/61–1929), also show the use of swags, fluting and the Vitruvian scroll, as on the Osterley tables.

The legs of these tables are similar to those of the chairs (E/1) and are, like them, echoed in the legs of Adam's steel grates.

E/3   LIBRARY DESK

Oak and pine, veneered with rosewood, satinwood and other woods; ormolu mounts; green baize top; leather castors. *En suite* with 2 tables (E/2) and 8 armchairs (E/1).
Height 79 cm. (31 in.).
O.P.H.263–1949.

The inventory of 1782 lists *A large curious inlaid Library Table covered with green Cloth richly ornamented with Or Molee with Drawers Doors locks and Keys*.

Of traditional form with Neo-Classical details, this desk bears some resemblance to the library table supplied by Chippendale to Harewood House (now at Temple Newsam, Leeds), by which it may have been influenced (illustrated in *MacQuoid and Edwards*, vol. III, p. 252, fig. 25). There is every reason to believe, however, that it was made in the same workshop as the rest of the furniture in this room, which is attributed to John Linnell. A feature which also suggests that Linnell was responsible for this piece is the erect acanthus leaf at the base of each stile, a motif seen on many pieces attributed to Linnell, such as the Library chairs (E/1), the furniture made for the Taffeta Bedroom at Osterley (Group L) and a cabinet (N/10).

The four doors of the pedestals are decorated respectively with emblems of Architecture, Sculpture, Painting and Music. The pedestals contain drawers and there are also drawers in the frieze, extending through the full width of the desk.

E/3

GROUP F

Osterley Park:
Furniture in the Drawing Room

The following pieces of furniture were probably all designed in about 1773 for the Drawing Room at Osterley Park, Middlesex. Adam's design for the pier-glasses, dated 1773, is on show at the house and there are designs by him for various parts of the commodes, one of which is dated 1773, at the Soane Museum. Although no designs exist for the candlestands, it is reasonable to assume on stylistic grounds that they were also designed by Adam. The room is known to have been completed by the summer of 1773, when Horace Walpole first visited the house, so that it seems probable that they were, like the commodes and pier-glasses, designed in that year. The seat furniture on the other hand, was probably both designed and made by John Linnell at about the same time.

A pole fire-screen (H/7) was listed as being in this room in the inventory of 1782. It has not been grouped with the Drawing Room furniture in this Catalogue, however, but in Group H, comprising the furniture for the State Bedroom, to which it is stylistically related.

F/1   COMMODE

Veneered with harewood, satinwood, rosewood
and other woods, some stained green; ormolu
mounts.

One of a pair.

Height 90 cm. (35½ in.).

O.P.H.82–1949.

The Inventory of 1782 lists *Two very Elegant
Eliptic Commodes with brass Ornaments gilt in
Gold and very curiously inlaid and leather
covers.*

This commode and its pair stand under the
pier-glasses (F/2) between the windows in the
Drawing Room. There is a design for the front
of the commode in the Soane Museum (vol. 18,
no. 58), without inscription or date, part of

which is shown in pl. F/1a. There are, however,
pencil annotations to the effect that the figures
were to be painted on a dark green ground. The
colouring of the design for the top also suggests
that the pattern was to be executed in paint
rather than in marquetry. This design (Soane
Museum, vol. 18, no. 63; pl. F/1b) is dated
30 January 1773, and is inscribed *Top of
Commode for Robert Child Esqr.* The other
designs are all undated. Vol. 25, no. 56 (pl.
F/1c) shows the central roundel, left-hand
candelabrum and frieze and is inscribed *Part of
Commode for Robert Child Esqr.* The roundel
of this drawing depicts Neptune, Juno and
Jupiter. The commodes were respectively
executed with Diana and her hounds and with
Venus and Cupid in their roundels. Two other

drawings (vol. 25, no. 210 and vol. 5, nos. 20 and 21) are for ornaments of the side panels, no. 20 being the design executed. Vol. 24, no. 238, a decorative detail of urn and scrolls, may possibly have been for this commode. Moreover, vol. 18, nos. 67 to 76 and no. 80 are all apparently preliminary sketches for the scenes depicted on the two commodes, whilst nos. 97 and 98 are for the griffins on the central mounts.

A semi-circular commode, similar in many respects, was designed by Adam, also in January 1773, for the Duke of Bolton (Soane Museum, vol. 17, no. 18; illustrated in *Harris*, pl. 44).

The use of inlaid strips of green-stained wood, as in the frame of the central roundel, is seen in other furniture in the house believed to be by Linnell, notably in the satinwood furniture made for the Taffeta Bedroom at Osterley (Group L).

Having no doors, this piece is purely ornamental and may be considered, like the pier-glasses, as being part of the wall-decoration. The design of the frieze (with acanthus scrolls and urns in marquetry, centring on the very fine ormolu tablet of a portrait medallion flanked by griffins) is repeated in the frieze over each of the doors in this room, in carved, painted and gilded wood. The design is echoed again in the marble chimneypiece but the portrait is replaced by an urn and the griffins by winged sphinxes. The motif of a medallion flanked by griffins had no doubt been seen by Adam in the Villa Madama, Rome, where he made a number of sketches of decorative details adapted by Raphael and Giovanni da Udine from Classical Roman originals.

Mr Colin Streeter of the Metropolitan Museum, New York, has pointed out that a commode of Neo-Classical design from the collection of the 5th Earl Temple, sold at Sotheby's on 9 May 1941, lot 101, bears a roundel depicting Diana similar to the one on the Osterley commode except that the hound on the left has been omitted.

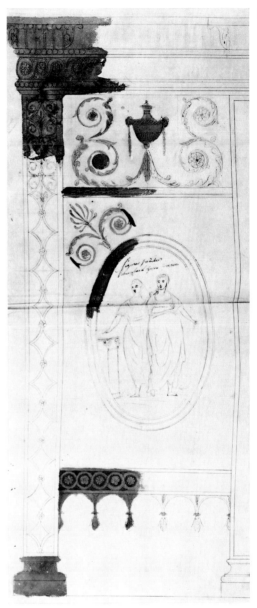

F/1a

F/1b

F/1c

F/2

F/2 PIER-GLASS
Frame of gilded pine.
One of a pair.
Height 340 cm. (134 in.).
O.P.H.79–1949.

The inventory of 1782 lists *Two very large
Pier Glasses the frames richly Carved and gilt
in burnish Gold the Plates Ninety nine by fifty
five Inches.*

This glass and its pair hang above the
commodes, between the windows. The design,
which is on show at Osterley, is dated 21 July
1773. There is also a design at the Soane
Museum (vol. 20, no. 34), inscribed *Design of a
Glass frame for the Drawing Room at
Osterly*, dated 1767, and a preliminary
drawing (vol. 20, no. 35). The Soane designs
are quite different from that at the house and
were not executed for Osterley.

If, as is suggested, the seat furniture and
commodes in this room were made by John
Linnell, these pier-glasses probably also came
from his workshop.

Mirror glass of such a large size was still not
being produced in this country at this date (but
see H/4), so these plates are presumably
French. (The transport of such large sheets of
glass must have presented considerable
problems.)

F/3

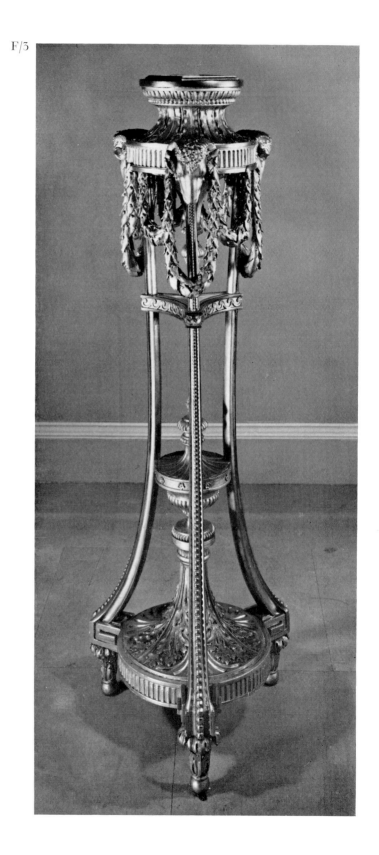

F/3 CANDLESTAND
Gilded pine and beech.
Height 144.5 cm. (57 in.).
O.P.H.83–1949.

The inventory of 1782 lists *Two Elegant Or Molee tripods*. Although these two candlestands are entirely of gilded wood, without any ormolu, one must assume that this discrepancy was due to a mistake on the part of the valuer. They are not mentioned elsewhere in the inventory and there are no other candlestands at Osterley answering to the description of 'Ormolu tripods'.

The tripod candlestand was an item of furniture much favoured by Adam and the overall design, as well as the individual motifs, leave little doubt that he was the designer.

F/4 ARMCHAIR

Gilded oak and beech; the upholstery, modern.
One of a set of 8. *En suite* with 2 settees (F/5).
Height 103.5cm. (40¾ in.).
O.P.H.88–1949.

The inventory of 1782 lists *Eight large Elbow
Chairs carved and gilt in burnish Gold covered
with pea green Silk Damask linen and serge
cases to the whole.*

Although this armchair is in the Rococo style,
rather than the Neo-Classical, it is included in
this book because it forms an intrinsic part of
the furnishings of the State Rooms at Osterley.
Adam probably was aware that at this date
it was customary in Paris to have chairs in
a slightly stiffened Rococo style in interiors
that otherwise were strictly Neo-Classical in
taste. Sets of chairs in this style were also
supplied to other houses that he was decorating
and furnishing at about the same time. For the
set supplied to Shardeloes, Buckinghamshire,
there is a bill from John Linnell, dated 27 July
1768, for *8 French chairs* and *2 sophas to match
the Chairs* (the chairs are now at Clarence
House). The set at Alnwick Castle (12
armchairs and 2 settees) is virtually identical
to the Osterley set. The connections that
Linnell had with both the Duke of Northumberland and Robert Child (see under E/2),
corroborate the contention that he was the
designer and maker of the sets at Alnwick and
Osterley. There is, moreover, a design amongst
his drawings in the Museum's Department of
Prints and Drawings (E.93–1929; pl. F/4a) on
which this chair appears to have been based.
Still more supporting evidence is supplied by a
comparison with some of the carved details on
the chimney-piece at Osterley (M/6), also
attributed to Linnell.

The Alnwick armchairs were attributed to
Thomas Chippendale in the Exhibition
*Thomas Chippendale and his Patrons in the
North*, Temple Newsam, 1968 (catalogue no.
15, pl. 3), where a pair of them was shown.
This attribution is based on the facts that they
are in a style represented in the *Director* and

V. A. M.

F/4a

that Chippendale dedicated the first edition, of
1754, to Hugh, Earl of Northumberland. On
the other hand, it should be noted that the
chairs for Alnwick and Osterley were not made
until 10 to 20 years later. Even so, despite the
evidence that so strongly favours the attribution
of the Osterley set to Linnell, the possibility
that they were made by Chippendale cannot be
entirely ruled out and it should be noted that
the two lacquer commodes at the house (I/1
and I/2), are tentatively attributed to him.

F/5   SETTEE
Gilded oak and beech; the upholstery, modern.
One of a pair. *En suite* with 8 armchairs (F/4).
Height 106 cm. (41¾ in.).
O.P.H.86–1949.

The inventory of 1782 lists *Two large Soffas
carved and gilt in burnish Gold with bolsters
covered with pea green Silk Damask.*

For further details, see under F/4, above.

F/5

GROUP G

Osterley Park:
Furniture in the Tapestry Room

The following suite of furniture was designed
for the Tapestry Room at Osterley Park,
Middlesex. The design for the room as a whole
was conceived by Robert Adam and may be
compared with similar tapestry rooms designed
by him, notably that at Newby Hall, Yorkshire,
and that at Croome Court, Worcestershire, now
removed to the Metropolitan Museum, New
York. Designs by Robert Adam exist for the
pier-glass and side-table, dated 1775, and for
the tripod candlestands, dated 1776. The
Gobelins tapestries are signed by Nielson, the
director of the tapestry works, and dated 1775.
Their collection from London on 5 July 1776
is recorded in an account at the Victoria and
Albert Museum *for ye Waggon to London for
ye tapestry 1s. 3d.* (E. Harris, ' Robert Adam
and the Gobelins', *Apollo*, April 1962, p. 100).

G/1 ARMCHAIR

Gilded beech and oak; upholstered in Gobelins tapestry.

One of a set of 8. *En suite* with a settee (G/2).

Height 95 cm. (37½ in.).

O.P.H.59–1949.

The inventory of 1782 lists *Eight Cabriole Chairs to match ditto* [*the settee*] *and linen and Serge Cases to all.*

The chairs are upholstered in tapestry with a crimson ground, like the wall-hangings, their oval backs echoing the medallions of the latter, which portray scenes from Boucher's 'Loves of the Gods'. The chair-backs illustrate Boucher's series *Les Enfants jardiniers,* whilst the seat-covers are decorated with floral bouquets after designs by Maurice Jacques and Charles Tessier.

The chairs were probably made shortly after the delivery of the tapestries in 1776. There is no design by Adam for these chairs and it seems probable, as suggested by *Harris*, p. 96, that their basic design originated in France and was interpreted in England. As Mrs Harris says, 'This is corroborated by the rounded seat, a feature that is well-known in France, for instance on *fauteuils à la Reine*, but is rare in England where the slightly serpentined or shaped rail is normally preferred. The rounded, fluted legs are also more characteristic of Louis XVI than English furniture. On the other hand, the splaying of the rear legs is a typically English custom not practised in France.' Adam makes use of the oval back again in the following year, 1777, for the State Bedroom chairs at Osterley (H/3), for which his design exists. He also designed armchairs with oval backs and rounded seats for Sir Abraham Hume in 1779. A significant point is that the construction of the Tapestry Room chairs is identical with that of the State Bedroom chairs, which must have been made in England, and quite different from French chairs of this type.

It may well be that John Linnell, who appears to have been responsible for many of the other chairs in the house, was the maker of this set.

G/2   SETTEE

Gilded beech and oak; upholstered in Gobelins tapestry. *En suite* with the set of 8 armchairs (G/1).
Height 111 cm. (43¾ in.).
O.P.H.58–1949.

The inventory of 1782 lists *A large Elegant Cabriole Soffa richly carved & gilt in burnish Gold and covered with Gobelin Tapestry.*

The settee may be related to a design by John Linnell in the Department of Prints and Drawings (E.123–1929) for a settee with a similar back, ornamented with the motif of trailing husks 'threaded through' the top-rail. The cartouche panel would appear to have been designed for a settee having a back of this shape, which was common in France, though seldom used in England (an example, however, is the settee made by Ince and Mayhew for the Tapestry Room at Croome Court). The adaptation of the basic design would have necessitated the addition of the bouquets of flowers to fill the empty space at either end.

G/3   TRIPOD STAND

Gilded beech and pine, with painted plaques. One of a pair.
Height 127 cm. (50 in.).
O.P.H.67–1949.

The inventory of 1782 lists *Two exceeding elegant tripod stands richly carved and gilt in burnish gold with three oval Paintings and green baize Covers.*

The design, in the Soane Museum (vol. 17, no. 62; pl. G/3a), is inscribed *Design of a Tripod for the Tapestry room at Osterly* and dated 13 November 1776. A tripod of very similar form was designed by Adam in 1773 for Sir Watkin Wynn's house in St James's Square. A tripod made to this design is now at Alnwick Castle, Northumberland. In these tripods, however, the side panels are decorated in relief, in contrast to the open-work carving and painted panels of the Osterley pair (*Harris*, pl. 137). Closely resembling the design for Sir Watkin Wynn was another for Lady Home, dated 1778, though in this the

G/2

rams' heads are replaced by lions' heads and the pedestal is supported on griffins instead of sphinxes (*Musgrave*, fig. 20).

The tripod pedestal derives ultimately from the form of the classical incense burner, which had been revived by James Stuart in about 1759 for Spencer House, London.

G/3a

G/3

G/4   SIDE-TABLE

Gilded pine and beech, with painted plaques;
the top of inlaid marble.
Height 88.9 cm. (35 in.).
O.P.H.57–1949.

The inventory of 1782 lists *A rich Carved and
gilt Eliptic Pier table frame with three painted
figures on the Rail* and *A Statuary Marble Slab
with rich Scagliola ornaments. A leather cover
lined*.

Designed to stand below the pier-glass,
between the windows. The design, in the
Soane Museum (vol. 17, no. 8), is inscribed
*Table frame and Slab for the Tapestry room at
Osterly* and dated 18 March 1775.

The top is made of marble inlaid with coloured
composition in a technique known as 'Bossi
work', after an Italian craftsman who
specialized in this work in Dublin. A similar
technique is used for the chimney-piece in
this room. The anthemion border of the table
top is repeated as a border in both the ceiling
and the carpet and the fan motif seen at the
centre of the table top appears again at the
corners of the ceiling and the carpet. The
painted plaques are a visual link with those on
the tripod pedestals.

G/4

G/5 PIER-GLASS
Frame of gilded and painted pine.
Height 269 cm. (106 in.).
O.P.H.54–1949.

The inventory of 1782 lists *A large Pier Glass
in an Elegant Carved and gilt frame the top
ornamented with figures and festoons of
flowers the Plate Ninety six by fifty six Inches.*

Designed for the pier between the windows.
The design, which is in the Soane Museum
(vol. 20, no. 43), is inscribed *Design of
a Glass frame for the Tapestry room at
Osterly* and dated 28 November 1775. Design
no. 42 is identical except that the figures are
unclothed (pl. G/5a).

G/5

G/5a

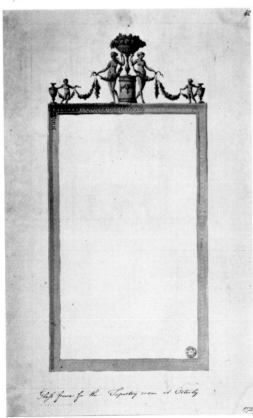

G/6   FIRE-SCREEN
Gilded mahogany and pine, with a panel of
Gobelins tapestry.
Height 132 cm. (52 in.).
O.P.H.71–1949.

The inventory of 1782 lists (as having been in
the South Passage, not the Tapestry Room) *An
Elegant Gobelin Tapestry fire screen in a gilt
frame and serge cover.*

It seems scarcely conceivable that this rather
coarse screen can be the 'Elegant Gobelin
Tapestry fire screen' of the inventory. The
present screen is made from a panel of tapestry
taken from the hanging behind the pier-glass,
the gap behind the glass having been made
good with plain material. Possibly the original
screen was damaged by fire and the present
one made to replace it, using a piece of tapestry
from a part of the wall where it would not be
seen.

G/6

GROUP H

Osterley Park:
Furniture in the State Bedroom

The following group of furniture was designed
by Robert Adam for the State Bedroom at
Osterley Park, Middlesex.

The designs date from 1775 (the pier-glass) to
1778 (the chimney-board). No design exists for
the pole-screen but it would appear to have
been designed by Adam at about the same time.
The maker may well have been John Linnell.

The commode is not included in this group, as
it is unlikely to have been designed by Adam
(see Group I).

H/1a

H/1 BEDSTEAD

Oak, beech and pine, painted and gilded; the hangings of olive green velvet and pale green silk, with embroidery in silver and silk of various colours, with yellow fringe and tassels. Height 445 cm. (175 in.).
O.P.H.29–1949.

The inventory of 1782 lists *A very Elegant State Bedstead with Eight painted & Japanned Columns with carved and gilt Capitals and bases on Inlaid Pedestals. A rich Carved and gilt Cornice and dome Teaster richly Carved and gilt. A Rich Japanned & highly carved and gilt headboard with figures and other ornaments the furniture Velvet Drapery richly embroidered in Colours the Dome and inside lined with green Silk embroidered in festoons and other ornaments the whole fringed in festoons with rich Gold colour Silk fringe and Tassells. A very elegant silk Counterpane richly embroidered with borders and compartments which terminate in festoons fringed with Tassells. A Silk Shade to throw over ditto.*

In the Soane Museum is a drawing dated 16 May 1776 (vol. 17, no. 157; pl. H/1a), inscribed *Design of a Bed for Robert Child Esqr.*, which corresponds to the actual bed. An earlier design (vol. 17, no. 156), dated 11 October 1775, differs slightly in the treatment of the tester and dome and is shown with pale blue hangings of a different form. Two further designs (vol. 17, nos. 158 and 159) are for the interior of the dome and for the counterpane, respectively.

The valance is decorated on alternate panels with an eagle holding an adder in its beak, the crest of the Child family, and a marigold, the symbol of the banking house of Child. The inside of the dome is also lined with silk, embroidered in various colours. On his visit in 1778, Horace Walpole described the bed as, 'too like a modern head-dress, for round the outside of the dome are festoons of artificial flowers'. These artificial flowers no longer exist. He also added the comment, 'What would Vitruvius think of a dome decorated by a milliner?'

The design appears to have been inspired by the Choragic Monument of Lysicrates, which was illustrated by James Stuart in *The Antiquities of Athens*, vol. I, published in 1762 (pl. H/1b); a copy of this monument was erected by Stuart in about 1769 at Shugborough Park, Staffordshire. Not only is the general form of a cupola upheld by columns common to both the monument and the bed but, in addition, most of the decorative details of the former have been re-interpreted in the design of the bed. The most obvious of these are the acroteria surmounting the entablature and the supporting dolphins, which originally surmounted the monument (pl. H/1c) and which reappear in the headboard of the bed. (See also the lantern, M/2.)

The four female sphinxes at the corners of the cornice are carved with charming naturalism in a manner reminiscent of mid-eighteenth-century French practice. Possibly a French immigrant carver may have been responsible. At any rate, the style is very different from that normally associated with English carving of this period.

H/1b

H/1c

H/2 PIER-GLASS

Frame of gilded and painted pine.
Height 243.8 cm. (96 in.).
O.P.H.34–1949.

The inventory of 1782 lists *A Pier Glass in a rich carved and gilt frame enclosing a Painting the Plate ninety two by fifty two Inches.*

H/2

The design for this glass, in the Soane Museum (vol. 20, no. 47; pl. H/2a), is inscribed *Glass frame for the Bed Chamber at Osterly* and dated 1775. A second design (vol. 20, no. 46), dated 15 May 1775, differs slightly in the details of the top.

Since the inspiration for the State Bed apparently comes from the Choragic Monument of Lysicrates, it seems likely that the surmounting pedestal on the pier-glass derives from the same source, for there was a tripod stand surmounting the monument (pl. H/1c).

The addorsed winged sphinxes on the pier-glass echo those on the chairs, on the chimney-board and at each corner of the bed. The painted plaque depicts Venus and Cupid.

In the entry for the pier-glasses in the Drawing Room (F/2) attention was drawn to the problems involved in making and transporting such large sheets of glass at that time. But see H/4 below.

H/2a

Glass frame for the Bed Chamber at Osterly.

H/3 ARMCHAIR

Gilded oak and beech; the upholstery, modern.
One of a set of 6.
Height 101 cm. (39¾ in.).
O.P.H.42–1949.

The inventory of 1782 lists *Six Cabriole Chairs richly Carved and gilt in burnish Gold covered with green Velvet flannel and serge cases to ditto*.

The design for these chairs, in the Soane Museum (vol. 17, no. 97; pl. H/3a), is inscribed *Design of a Chair for the Bed Chamber at Osterly* and dated 24 April 1777. The upholstery is shown as being mottled and coloured bluish-green.

The use of the winged sphinx, one of Adam's favourite motifs, as a support for the oval back is an unusual and attractive feature of this chair. It is echoed in the sphinx surmounting each corner of the bed and in the addorsed sphinxes at the top of the pier-glass and on the chimney-board.

H/3a

H/4　CHIMNEY-GLASS

Frame of gilded and painted pine and beech.
Height 308.5 cm. (121½ in.).
O.P.H.35–1949.

The inventory of 1782 lists *A Chimney Glass
in a rich Carved and gilt frame with Cupids and
festoons enclosing a Painting the Plate Ninety
six by sixty Inches. 1st plate made in England.*

As in the pier-glass in this room, the painted
plaque represents Venus and Cupid. The
surmounting motif of an eagle with an adder
in its beak, the crest of the Child family, also
appears in the valance of the bed.

The statement in the 1782 inventory that this
was the first plate made in England presumably
means that this was the first of the very large
plates of glass at Osterley to have been made in
this country, and that the slightly earlier ones
in the Drawing Room and the Tapestry Room,
and perhaps the pier-glass in the Bed-Chamber,
had all been imported from France (F/2, G/5
and H/2). Such large plates of glass had, in any
case, only recently become available at that
time.

H/5　CHIMNEY-BOARD

Painted canvas on a wooden frame; brass
handle.
Height 117 cm. (46 in.).
O.P.H.28–1949.

The inventory of 1782 lists *A chimney board
covered with Paper painted with Etruscan
ornaments.*

The design for this, in the Soane Museum (vol.
17, no. 138; pl. H/5a), is inscribed *Chimney
Board for the Bed Chamber at Osterly* and
dated 22 August 1778. It is in colour. There is
an identical design in black and white (vol. 17,
no. 139), which is similarly inscribed.

Fire-places had been blocked by various means
in the past, during the season when fires were
not necessary. Panels of tapestry, gilt leather,
iron, and painted paper stretched on a wooden
frame were by no means uncommon in the

H/4

seventeenth century. Adam designed such 'chimney-boards' for the rooms at Osterley where draughts from the chimney would have been particularly undesirable—the Bedroom and the Dressing Room (J/2).

The tripod pedestal motif, used on top of the pier-glass in this room, appears again in the design of this chimney-board. The theme of 'Sleep', represented in the painted lunette in the style of Angelica Kauffmann, is repeated in an oval plaque in the centre of the ceiling.

H/5a

H/5

H/6   POLE-SCREEN

Gilded beech; the panel of white satin, embroidered with gold, silver and coloured silks.

Of the same design as pole-screen H/7, except for the panel.

Height 157.5cm. (62in.).

O.P.H.41–1949.

Unaccountably, the inventory of 1782 makes no mention of this pole-screen although the similar one (H/7) is listed (as having been in the Drawing Room). There is no reason, however, to doubt that both were made at about the same time. There is no design in existence for either of the two pole-screens but the general form and lightness suggest an Adam design of the late 1770s, when the rest of the State Bedroom furniture was designed. Moreover, the combination of paterae and strings of husks on the tripod base is found again in the chimney-piece, in the chimney-board and at the tops of the chairs, such a repetition of motifs often being used by Adam to link different pieces of furniture in a room. The acanthus carving on the legs is also very like the same decoration on the arm supports of the chairs.

The panel has an embroidered design of a monogram, *S.C.* This is obviously the work of an unskilled hand and may have been done by Sarah Anne Child, Robert's daughter, who was born in 1764.

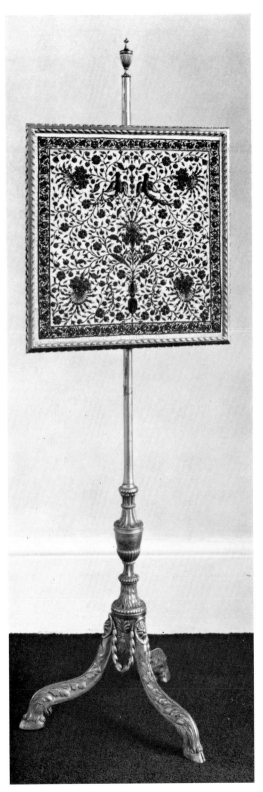

H/7

H/7   POLE-SCREEN

Gilded beech; the panel of white satin embroidered with gold, silver and coloured silks.

Of the same design as pole-screen H/6, except for the panel.

Height 157.5 cm. (62 in.).

O.P.H.40–1949.

The inventory of 1782 lists, as having been in the Drawing Room, *A carved and gilt in burnish Gold pole fire Screen covered with Needlework and Serge Covers for Ditto.*

The expression, 'covered with Needlework', in the inventory suggests that this screen, which has an overall design, is referred to, rather than the oval-panelled screen (H/6), which does not appear to have been listed (see above). It was presumably made at the same time as the other screen, ie contemporaneously with the furniture for the State Bedroom (rather than the Drawing Room), when Adam had adopted a lighter, more delicate, style. It seems probable that, after the pole-screen had been made for the Bedroom, it was decided that a similar one would be desirable for the Drawing Room but it was not thought necessary to produce an entirely new design.

GROUP I

Osterley Park:
Lacquer Commodes from the State Bedroom
and the Etruscan Room

No designs exist for the two commodes
discussed below. They are mentioned in the
1782 inventory of Osterley Park as belonging
respectively in the State Bedchamber and the
Etruscan Dressing Room. Most of the furniture
in these rooms (with the exception of the
table, J/5), was designed by Adam between
about 1775 and 1778 but the character of these
two commodes suggests that a different
designer was responsible for their conception.
Adam favoured rectangular or semi-circular
plan-forms for side-tables and commodes (see
the Drawing Room commode, F/1, and the
Tapestry Room side-table, G/4, for example)
but the plan of these two pieces is irregular
and reminiscent of that found in commodes
believed to be by Thomas Chippendale. The
peg-top feet are also of a type found on
furniture thought to be by Chippendale.
Moreover, the individual decorative motifs
found on each commode, while they echo
those of the Bedchamber and the Dressing
Room, respectively, are not treated in exactly
the same way as those in the rooms and on the
rest of the furniture there. This, too, suggests
that a different designer was responsible for
the commodes, although Adam presumably
gave general instructions for their design.
Although Chippendale is not known to have
supplied furniture to Robert Child, he
certainly worked for Adam, who is known to
have sent him sketches that Chippendale,
himself no mean draughtsman, then worked
up into practical designs (see A/1).

A further notable feature that sets these two
commodes apart from the rest of the furniture
in the rooms where they stand is the fact that
both are veneered with Oriental lacquer. Adam
is not known ever to have designed furniture

in the Chinese taste although Chippendale
produced furniture in this exotic vein for other
houses under Adam's general supervision (in
the State Bedroom at Nostell Priory, Yorkshire,
for instance). The introduction into these
otherwise completely Neo-Classical rooms of
Oriental decoration is somewhat surprising,
especially in the case of the Dressing Room,
where the contrast with the Etruscan style is
particularly incongruous. Robert Child,
however, seems to have had a liking for this
exotic style and several other rooms in the
house contained items of Oriental furniture,
as well as textiles of Chinese origin (as, for
instance, those used on the bed and chairs from
the Taffeta Bedroom, L/1 and L/2).

I/1 COMMODE

Japanned and gilded oak and pine, inset with panels of Oriental lacquer and embellished with carved and gilded wood simulating ormolu mounts; brass handles.
Height 91.4cm. (36in.).
O.P.H.36–1949.

Part of the furnishing of the State Bedroom.

The inventory of 1782 lists *A large Japanned Commode with gilt Ornaments*.

The short legs terminating in block feet are closely similar to those on the dressing-commode supplied by Chippendale to Harewood House in 1773 (*Musgrave*, pl. 121), and on the pair of china-cabinets attributed to him at Firle Place, Sussex (*Musgrave*, pl. 172). The decoration of the stiles in gilded wood is a simplification of the ormolu mounts of rams' heads and pendent husks within frames used on the library table Chippendale supplied to Harewood House (*Musgrave*, pl. 167). (The rams' heads and trailing husks are echoed in the chimney-piece of the Osterley State Bedroom.) Similarly, the half patera at the head of each stile of this commode is used by Chippendale on the dressing-table he supplied for the Amber Room at Nostell Priory.

I/1

I/2   COMMODE

Japanned and gilded oak and pine, inset with
panels of Oriental lacquer and embellished
with carved and gilded wood simulating
ormolu mounts; brass handles.
Height 89 cm. (35 in.).
O.P.H.37–1949.

Part of the furnishing of the Etruscan
Dressing Room.

The inventory of 1782 lists *A large Japanned
commode with carved ornaments gilt and leather
Cover*.

The commode resembles, in outline and in the
form of the legs, the japanned commode in the
State Bedroom at Nostell Priory, which is
believed to have been supplied by Chippendale
in about 1771 (*Musgrave*, pl. 120).

The lion's head motif on this commode is
echoed on the base of the tripod pole-screen
(J/4), and, in paint, on the armchairs in this
room (J/1).

Another very similar commode was formerly in
the collection of the Earl of Dundonald
(present whereabouts unknown).

I/2

GROUP J

Osterley Park:
Furniture in the Etruscan Room

The following group of furniture was designed
by Robert Adam for the Etruscan Room at
Osterley Park, Middlesex.

Adam claimed that 'A mode of Decoration has
been here attempted, which differs from
anything hitherto practised in Europe; for
although the style of the ornament and the
colouring . . . are both evidently imitated from
the vases and urns of the Etruscans, yet we
have not been able to discover, either in our
researches into antiquity or in the works of
modern artists, any idea of applying this taste
to the decoration of apartments' (*Adam*, vol. II,
Preface. Adam is actually referring to Old
Derby House in Grosvenor Square but his
remarks apply equally well to Osterley). The
vases and urns referred to, believed at that
time to be Etruscan, were, in fact, Greek. The
decoration of the Etruscan Room is only
faintly suggestive of Greek vase paintings,
however, the figures lacking the flatness of
those on Greek pottery, while the surrounding
ornament bears a closer resemblance to Roman
and Renaissance grotesques.

The room served as a dressing room for the
adjoining State Bedroom. The designs for the
furniture were made during the years 1775 to
1779 inclusive.

J/1 ARMCHAIR

Beech, painted in terracotta-colour and black
on a grey ground; cane seat, with a grey silk
squab cushion.
One of a set of 8.
Height 90.8 cm. (35¾ in.).
O.P.H.10–1949.

The inventory of 1782 lists *Eight Elbow Chairs
japanned with Etruscan ornaments highly
varnished and polished Cane Seats and Cushions
covered with grey silk bordered and bound with
Silk Lace Gimp and fringe & Stripe Cases.*

The design, in the Soane Museum (vol. 17, no.
95; pl. J/1a), is inscribed *Chair for the Etruscan
room at Osterly*, and dated 6 March 1776. An
earlier design (vol. 17, no. 96; pl. J/1b) shows
arms in the form of griffins. It is dated 25
January 1776 and inscribed *A Design of a Chair
for the Etruscan Dressing Room at Osterly.*

In 1775 Adam had designed a somewhat
similar Etruscan armchair for Lord Stanley,
which had terracotta-coloured ornaments on a
black ground (vol. 17, no. 94).

J/1a

J/1b

J/2 CHIMNEY-BOARD

Painted canvas on a wooden frame; brass handle.

Height 117 cm. (46 in.).

O.P.H.5–1949.

The inventory of 1782 specifies of the Etruscan Dressing Room that *The Room [is] hung with Canvas and Paper and very elegantly painted with Etruscan ornaments and Chimney board ditto.*

The design, in the Soane Museum (vol. 17, no. 137; pl. J/2a), is inscribed *Chimney board for the Etruscan Dressing room at Osterly*, and dated 2 June 1777. There is also a pen and ink sketch (vol. 24, no. 221; pl. J/2b) which shows an alternative composition on the right-hand side.

J/2a

J/2b

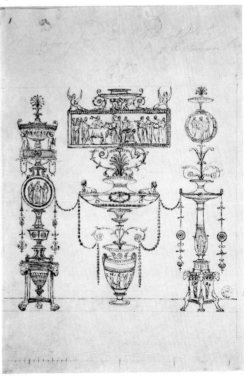

J/3   PIER-GLASS

The frame of pine, painted black and partly
gilded, with a painted plaque in various colours.
Height 233.7 cm. (92 in.).
O.P.H.8–1949.

The inventory of 1782 lists *A large Elegant
Glass the frame carved and gilt in burnish
Gold enclosing a Painting the Plate Ninety two
by fifty two inches.*

The design, in the Soane Museum (vol. 17,
no. 44), is inscribed *Glass Frame for the
Etruscan Dressing room at Osterly* and dated
15 May 1775. A second design (vol. 17, no. 45;
pl. J/3a) is virtually identical. If the note in the
1782 inventory concerning the chimney-glass
in the State Bedroom is correct (see H/4), then
the plate for this glass must have been
imported from France.

J/3a

J/3

J/4 POLE-SCREEN

Beech, painted in terracotta-colour and black on a grey ground; panel of embroidered silk within a gilded moulding.
Height 167.6 cm. (66 in.).
O.P.H.18–1949.

The inventory of 1782 lists *A Tripod fire Screen Japanned to match covered with Needlework & Silk back.*

The tripod stand is based, with some modifications, on a design in the Soane Museum (vol. 17, no. 148), dated 30 April 1779 and inscribed *Fire Screen for Mrs. Child.* The design for the panel (vol. 17, no. 145) is similarly inscribed and dated 14 April 1777. An undated design (vol. 17, no. 149) is inscribed *Copy of ornament upon the edge of Mrs. Child's firescreen.* Alternative designs that were not executed include vol. 17, nos. 141, 142 and 143, dating from November and December 1776, and vol. 17, nos. 135 and 136, dated 4 November 1779.

The classical tripod, here headed with lion masks, is used for the base of the stand and the motif is repeated in the painted decoration of the walls. The shaft is in the form of a thyrsus. The stand is a most delicately conceived and executed piece of work.

Since the references on the designs are to Mrs Child, rather than to Robert Child, it may be that she embroidered the panel.

J/5   PEMBROKE TABLE

Mahogany, painted in ivory on a black ground
and partly gilded; leather castors.
Height 74 cm. (29 in.).
O.P.H.25–1949.

The inventory of 1782 lists *A Pembroke table
richly Japanned by Clay*.

This piece of furniture was either designed for
the Etruscan Room or at least installed in it
soon after the room was completed. No design
exists for it and it does not appear to have been
designed by Adam.

The maker was presumably Henry Clay, who
specialized in japanned goods made of papier-
mâché and who is known to have supplied

trays made of this material for Lord Jersey at
Osterley in 1804 and 1807. He also supplied
some japanned trays for Syon House where, of
course, Adam was also working in the 1770s.
Henry Clay, who had premises in King Street,
Covent Garden, described himself on his trade
card as 'Japanner in Ordinary to His Majesty
and His Royal Highness The Prince of Wales'.
A visitor to Clay's factory in 1775 stated that
he made boxes, tea-caddies, panels for coaches
and sedan-chairs, coffee-trays and 'all kinds of
other vessels, black with orange figures in the
style of Etruscan vases' (*Georg Christoph
Lichtenberg's visits to England as described in
his letters and diaries*. Translated and anno-
tated by M. L. Mare and W. H. Quarrell.
Oxford, 1938).

J/5

GROUP K

Osterley Park:
Furniture in the Breakfast Room

The following pieces of furniture were made
for the Breakfast Room at Osterley Park,
Middlesex. The pier-glass and table were
designed by Robert Adam in 1777; the maker
is unknown. The armchairs were probably
designed and made by John Linnell at about
the same time. The settee appears to be by a
different maker and may be of a slightly later
date.

K/1

K/1   PIER-GLASS
Frame of gilded pine.
One of a pair. *En suite* with side-table, K/2,
above which it hangs.
Height 239 cm. (94 in.).
O.P.H.285–1949.

The inventory of 1782 lists *A pair of Elegant
glass bordered pier Glasses in rich Gold frames.*

A design in the Soane Museum (vol. 20, no. 49;
pl. K/1a) shows the pier-glass and table
together. It is inscribed *Glass and Table frame
for the Breakfasting room at Osterly* and is
dated 24 April 1777. A hinged flap shows an
alternative design for the top part of the glass
and it is from this second version that the work
was executed.

The attenuation and excessive delicacy of the
forms are typical of some of Adam's later
designs. It contrasts strongly with the pier-
glasses in the rooms on the South side of the
house, which are all in his earlier style,
although the design of the chimney-glass in the
State Bedroom (H/4) in fact only pre-dates it by
three days.

K/1a

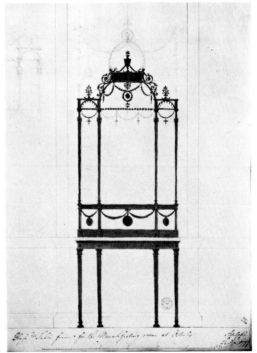

K/2

K/2   PIER-TABLE

Gilded pine, with a marble top.
One of a pair. *En suite* with pier-glass, K/1.
Height 84 cm. (33 in.).
O.P.H.283–1949.

The inventory of 1782 lists *A pair of Table frames gilt in oylgold with Marble Slabs.*

The design, in the Soane Museum (vol. 20, no. 49; pl. K/1a), shows the table and pier-glass together. It is inscribed *Glass and Table frame for the Breakfasting room at Osterly* and dated 24 April 1777.

Compared with Adam's earlier work in the house, there is a certain meanness and lack of inventiveness in the design of this table. The fluting of the legs and the frieze, combined with the use of paterae, echo these features on the chairs.

K/3 ARMCHAIR

Mahogany, upholstered in modern silk.
One of a set of 10. *En suite* with the settee, K/4.
Height 89 cm. (35 in.).
O.P.H.294–1949.

The inventory of 1782 lists *Ten Elegant Carved Elbow Mahogany Chairs covered with Needlework and Cases.*

Probably designed and made by John Linnell. There are points of resemblance to a number of designs by Linnell in the Victoria and Albert Museum; in particular, one design (E.82–1949) shows arms with an identical termination consisting of a ball or fruit with a collar of leaves. Further indication of Linnell's responsibility is given by the fact that there was formerly in one of the upper rooms at Osterley a set of mahogany armchairs (P. MacQuoid, *History of English furniture*, vol. IV, London and New York, 1908, fig. 95), which were identical to these except that they had backs very like those of the satinwood Library armchairs (E/1), for which designs by Linnell exist. Moreover, a set of armchairs having the same type of arm was designed by Linnell for Ammerdown, Somerset (*Musgrave*, p. 122).

The fluted legs and seat-rails, punctuated with paterae, are echoed in the pier-tables.

K/4 SETTEE

Mahogany, upholstered in modern silk.
En suite with the armchair K/3.
Height 92 cm. (36¼ in.).
O.P.H.304–1949.

The inventory of 1782 lists *A Mahogany Soffa to match in Canvas two bolsters and Stripe Cases.*

The sofa is rather spindly and is less well carved than the chairs. It is mentioned in the 1782 inventory but there is no obvious reason why a sofa should have been included among the furniture designed for a 'Breakfasting room' and it may be that this settee was added as an afterthought, perhaps provided by a less skilled craftsman than those working for Linnell. (The fact that the inventory lists a harpsichord as having been in the room in 1782 suggests that the room was by then no longer used as a breakfast room.)

K/4

GROUP L

Osterley Park:
Furniture from the Taffeta Bedroom

The following group of furniture is from the
Taffeta Bedroom at Osterley Park, Middlesex.
This is on the upper floor and is not one of the
State Rooms. The furniture is at present
displayed in a small room at the south-east
corner on the main floor.

There is a design by Robert Adam for the bed,
dated 1779. The frames of the pier-glass and of
the Chinese painting on glass may also be
attributed to him on stylistic grounds,
although no designs exist. The armchairs,
chest-of-drawers, night-tables and Pembroke
table, on the other hand, though designed *en
suite* with the bed, do not suggest the hand of
Adam and were perhaps designed and made by
John Linnell. The State Bedroom at Castle
Howard, Yorkshire, has furniture of very
similar design, which is also believed to be by
Linnell, although the author has seen no
documentary proof of this.

L/1

L/1 BEDSTEAD

Satinwood veneer, inlaid with green-stained wood; gilded carvings; hangings of Chinese painted taffeta with a design in dark green and other colours on a white ground.
Height 336.5 cm. (132½ in.).
O.P.H.314–1949.

The inventory of 1782 lists, under the *Yellow Taffaty Bed Chamber*, *A Rich Inlaid Satinwood Bedstead with inlaid and gilt Cornices painted Taffaty furniture lined with white silk green Silk fringe Tassells and festoons brass rod and green Silk Shade round Ditto*. The bed also had *A rich Satin Decca work Counterpane lined and fringed*, which no longer exists. This counterpane may have been of embroidery on satin of the type produced in the Deccan, in India. Considerable numbers of these were imported into this country, mainly in the seventeenth century, and the one mentioned may have been a family heirloom.

The design for this bed (Soane Museum, vol. 17, no. 163; pl. L/1a) is inscribed *Design of a Bed for Robert Child Esqr.* and dated 10 April 1779. The bed in the Castle Howard State Bedroom is of very similar form but has a domed top.

L/1a

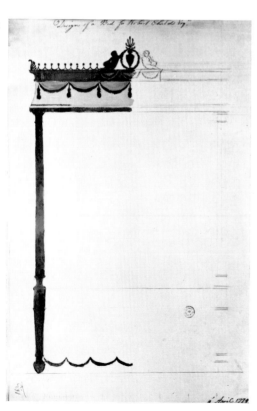

L/2 ARMCHAIR

Beechwood, painted to represent satinwood,
inlaid with green-stained wood; painted
ornament in green and black; squab cushion
covered with the same material as the bed
hangings.
One of a set of 13.
Height 93 cm. (36½ in.).
O.P.H.116–1949.

L/2

The inventory of 1782 lists *Nine Elbow
Satinwood Chairs inlaid and Japanned Cane
seats Cushions covered with Taffaty fringed to
match.* (The other four forming the set were
listed as being in the dressing room.)

There is no design for this chair but a design
by John Linnell in the Department of Prints
and Drawings (E.195–1929) has a back and
arms of a somewhat similar type. The armchairs belonging to the Castle Howard suite
(see p. 89) differ in having shield-backs but in
other respects closely resemble this chair.

It is interesting to note that there is a bill dated
January 1784 from John Linnell to Mrs Child
for *6 neat Sattin-wood Elbow Chairs with splat
Backs cut thro' matted Seats, Cushions to Do.*
The present satinwood chairs have splats 'cut
through'* and are fitted with matted seats but
it is of course not certain that these chairs were
of the same type as the 13 in the Taffeta
Bedroom and its adjoining dressing room,
which were all here by August 1782, when the
inventory was drawn up. Possibly Linnell
waited 16 months before sending Mrs Child a
bill for six of these chairs but, when one
considers how pressed the eighteenth-century
cabinet-makers usually were for ready cash,
this seems most unlikely. All the same, there
are no other chairs answering to this description
in the house.

*The words 'cut through' could, on the other
hand, refer to the 'matted Seats', drawing
attention to their drop-in construction, which is
unusual for cane seats.

L/3   NIGHT-TABLE

Oak and pine, veneered with satinwood,
cross-banded with rosewood and inlaid with
green-stained wood; brass handles. The drawer
contains a white ceramic pan beneath a
circular wooden lid.
One of a pair.
Height 83 cm. $(32\frac{3}{4}$ in.$)$.
O.P.H.310–1949.

The inventory of 1782 lists *Two inlaid
Satinwood commode and leather Cover*.

The pair of night-tables belonging to the suite
at Castle Howard have green painted decoration
on a satinwood veneer and tambour fronts, like
the Osterley pair, but the overall design is
rather different.

The erect acanthus leaf at the base of the stile
(and similarly on the chest-of-drawers *en suite*,
L/4) is to be found on a number of the pieces
attributed to Linnell (eg E/3). A further link
with Linnell is that the combination of pendent
husks, acanthus and marquetry fluting, used
in a vertical progression at the corners, repeats
in a slightly different form the decoration on
the stiles of a cabinet in the Museum collection
(N/10), which is based on a Linnell design.

L/3

L/4   CHEST-OF-DRAWERS

Oak and pine, veneered with satinwood,
cross-banded with rosewood and inlaid with
green-stained wood; brass handles.
Height 84·5 cm. $(33\frac{1}{4}$ in.$)$.
O.P.H.320–1949.

Strangely, there is no mention of a chest-of-
drawers in the Taffeta Bedroom in the inventory
of 1782. However, the shape and decorative
details of this piece closely follow the design of
the night-tables and there is every reason to
believe that they are all contemporary.

The honey-coloured satinwood, framed with
warm rosewood, and with touches of green
marquetry – combined with the meticulous
craftsmanship – makes this commode an
especially handsome piece of furniture in the
reticent vein for which English cabinet-makers
were famous at that time.

L/5   PEMBROKE TABLE

Oak, beech and pine, veneered with satinwood,
crossbanded with rosewood; brass mounts;
leather castors.
Height 71.5 cm. $(28\frac{1}{4}$ in.$)$.
O.P.H.72–1949.

The inventory of 1782 lists *A Satinwood
Pembroke Table*.

This piece differs from the furniture listed
above in that it has no decoration in green-
stained wood. However, it resembles the night-
tables and chest-of-drawers in the rosewood
cross-banding round the satinwood veneer.

L/4

L/5

L/6

L/6 PIER-GLASS

Frame of carved and gilded wood.
Height 211 cm. (83 in.).
O.P.H.308–1949.

The inventory of 1782 lists *A Pier Glass in an elegant carved and gilt in burnish Gold frame 24 by 34 head plate 10 by 24.*

This pier-glass was designed to hang between the windows, facing the fireplace, in the Taffeta Bedroom. Although there is but little in its design to relate it to the satinwood furniture from the same room, it echoes, in its central feature at the base, the gilded anthemion that surmounts each side of the canopy of the bed. Part of the cresting, which consisted of swags draped from carved ribbons at the top and sides, is now missing.

It now hangs in the Drawing Room.

L/7

L/7 PICTURE FRAME

Carved and gilded wood. (Framing a Chinese painting on glass.)
Height 124.5 cm. (49 in.).
O.P.H.313–1949.

The inventory of 1782 lists *An India Painting on Plate Glass with an elegant carved and gilt frame.*

This frame was designed to hang over the chimney-piece in the Taffeta Bedroom, facing the pier-glass (L/6), which it closely resembles. The anthemion at its base is almost identical with those surmounting the bed. It lacks part of its original decoration of carved ribbons and swags at the top.

It now hangs in the Breakfast Room.

GROUP M

Osterley Park:
Miscellaneous furniture at Osterley

This group consists of miscellaneous furniture
in the Adam style at Osterley Park.

M/1 LANTERN

Clear and green glass, mounted in ormolu; silk tassels.
One of a set of three.
Height 86.5cm. (34in.).
O.P.H.246–1949.

The inventory of 1782 lists *Three elegant Lamps mounted in Or Molee with brass ballance weights lines Tassells and double pullies Antique burners hung with Chains compleat.*

A sketch for these lanterns is in the Soane Museum (vol. 6, no. 60). One is reproduced in plate 8 of *Adam*, vol. III, 1822, together with several other Osterley pieces, where it is wrongly described as 'Furniture at Sion-house'. These lanterns and those comprising M/2 were probably executed at the Soho (Birmingham) factory of Matthew Boulton, the leading English maker of high-quality decorative metalwork at that time.

M/2 LANTERN

Clear and green glass, mounted in ormolu; base of gilded wood; modern fittings.
One of a pair.
Height 76cm. (30in.).
O.P.H.249–1949.

The inventory of 1782 lists *An Elegant Glass Lamp mounted with Or Molee ornaments and Antique Lamp with two burners* as having been on a pedestal (M/3) in the North Passage. The pair to it was on the *Great Stair Case*, also on a pedestal.

The lantern is illustrated, together with several other Osterley pieces, in *Adam*, vol. III, 1822, pl. 8, where it is wrongly described as 'Furniture at Sion-house', and shown as a hanging lantern. (Although it must obviously have had a stand when resting on a pedestal in 1782, the present base appears to be modern and may date from the time when the lantern was converted to electricity.) The design was probably executed at the Soho (Birmingham) factory of Matthew Boulton, the principal English maker of high-quality decorative metalwork at that time (see also M/1).

The supporting dolphins at the top appear to have been inspired by the same motif on the Choragic Monument of Lysicrates as illustrated by James Stuart in the *Antiquities of Athens*, vol. I, published in 1762 (pl. H/1c). A copy of this monument was erected by Stuart in the park at Shugborough, Staffordshire, in about 1769 and the dolphins on this were supplied by Matthew Boulton; this lends support to the belief that Boulton made the Osterley lanterns.

M/2

M/3

M/3   PEDESTAL
Carved pine, painted green and white.
One of a pair.
Height 120 cm. (47¼ in.).
O.P.H.251–1949.

The inventory of 1782 lists *A Tripod term painted green and white with an elegant glass Lamp*, etc., as being on the *Great Stair Case*, with a similar entry for the North Passage (for the lamp, see M/2).

Although no design exists for this pedestal, it can be attributed to Adam on stylistic grounds. The treatment of the top is not unlike that of the bracket in the Great Hall (B/2), whilst fluted legs, terminating in paw feet and surmounted by rams' heads are used, though in a different form, for the hall seats (B/1).

M/4

M/4 BEDSTEAD

Mahogany, oak and pine, the latter painted
green and white; green and white striped
silk lining the canopy.
Height 264 cm. (104 in.).
O.P.H.317–1949.

The inventory of 1782 lists as being in *Mr.
Child's Bed Chamber*, on the top floor, *A
Mahogany lath bottom four post Bedstead and
sweep carved cornices Decca work furniture
lined with green Silk fringed.*

No design exists for this bedstead. From the
decoration of the mahogany posts, it appears to
have been designed *en suite* with the set of
twelve armchairs formerly at the house, of
which the lower parts are similar to those of
the Breakfast Room armchairs (K/3). The 1782
inventory does, in fact, list six mahogany
chairs as having been in Mr Child's Bedchamber
and six in his dressing room and these may well
be identical with this set. Since the chairs are
believed to be by Linnell, this suggests that he
may also have made the bedstead.

The only part of the original hangings which
exists is a valance, which is of painted taffeta,
similar to that of the hangings of the satinwood
bedstead (L/1). The canopy is lined with green
and white striped silk underneath.

M/5

M/5 PLANT STAND or JARDINIÈRE

Pine, painted a terracotta colour on an ivory
ground; leather castors.
One of two similar stands.
Height 78 cm. (30¾ in.).
O.P.H.23–1949.

No design exists for these stands. The inventory
of 1782 lists *Two painted flower Stands* in the
Breakfast Room and two more in the Hall but
it seems unlikely that either of these two
stands, which are comparatively crude, can
have been made for such important rooms.
Both were formerly thought to have been part
of the original furnishings of the Etruscan
Dressing Room, since the colouring resembles
that of some of the other furniture in the room.
However, it is now believed that they may have
been designed for the Etruscan Grotto under
the staircase on the South-West, or Garden,
Front, because the decoration in fact echoes that
of the Grotto far more closely than that of the
Etruscan Room. Moreover, they fit the two
recesses in the Grotto.

The second stand, though intended as a pair to
the one illustrated, is not identical and shows
signs of having been made in the nineteenth
century, perhaps to replace one that had
become damaged. The painting on both stands
is identical and is apparently stencilled. This
suggests that, when the replacement was made,
both stands were painted (M/5 repainted) to
the original pattern, for the sake of uniformity.

M/6 CHIMNEY-PIECE AND GLASS
The chimney-piece is of white marble and carved wood, painted white; the glass has a frame of carved and gilded wood, with a pastel portrait.
Height 174 cm. (68½ in.).
O.P.H.361–1949.

The inventory of 1782 lists *An oval Glass bordered Chimney Glass in a Rich carved and gilt frame enclosing a Picture in crayons.*

This chimney-piece was made for Mrs Child's Dressing Room on the top floor. (The room is not open to the public.) There is a design for it by John Linnell in the Department of Prints and Drawings (E.281–1929; pl. M/6a) and it is reasonable to assume

that he was also the maker. It may be compared with the chairs and sofas made for the Drawing Room (F/4 and F/5) in that, like them, it is basically in the Rococo style having only a few details, such as the pendent husks, of Neo-Classical type. There is also a resemblance in the treatment of certain details to similar ones on the chairs, one example being the broken line running through the acanthus leaves at the base.

Another drawing by Linnell in the same volume (E.269–1929) appears to be a preliminary design for the same chimney-piece and is simply inscribed *Dressing Room.*

The portrait is said to be of Sarah Anne Child, Robert's daughter.

M/6

M/6a

GROUP N

Furniture by Adam or closely related to his work

This group consists of furniture designed by Adam and of other items closely related to his style, including three pieces based on designs by John Linnell and probably made at his workshop.

N/1   DOORWAY
Painted pine.
About 1770.
Height 353 cm. (139 in.).
Given by the National Art-Collections Fund.
W.44–1936.

This doorway comes from 10 Adelphi
Terrace, London, which was designed by
Robert and James Adam as part of their
speculative housing scheme on the bank of the
Thames.

The low relief decoration of the pilasters is
typical of Adam's work.

N/2   CHIMNEY-PIECE
Painted pine and marble.
About 1770.
Height 160 cm. (63 in.).
Given by the National Art-Collections Fund.
W.42–1936.

Designed by Adam in about 1770 for the
ground-floor front room at 5 Adelphi
Terrace, London, the house of David Garrick,
the actor. The ceiling from this room is also in
the Museum. The house was part of the Adam
Brothers' Adelphi development and Robert
Adam himself lived next door at no. 4.

N/3   CHIMNEY-GLASS
Frame of gilded pine.
About 1774.
Height 208 cm. (82 in.).
W.66–1938.

This glass was formerly in the Drawing Room
at Bradbourne, Kent, the room having been
decorated in 1774. An old photograph of the
chimney-glass *in situ* (*Country Life*, vol. XLIV,
24 August 1918, p. 157) shows the griffins
wrongly assembled and facing outwards.

In its details, though not in its pronouncedly
horizontal form, this glass is strongly
influenced by Adam.

N/1

N/4

N/4   CABINET
Mahogany and oak, veneered with rosewood,
satinwood and other woods, some stained
green; decoration in red and blue paint; inset
with panels of marble and landscapes of
marble intarsia; ormolu mounts.
1771/75.
Height 188.5 cm. (74¼ in.).
W.43–1949.

The cabinet was designed by Adam for the
Duchess of Manchester's country seat,
Kimbolton Castle, Huntingdonshire. The
design was executed in 1775 by the firm of Ince
and Mayhew, the mounts being supplied by
Messrs Boulton and Fothergill of Soho,
Birmingham. It was made in order to display
the Florentine marble intarsia panels
depicting landscapes. The only access to the
interior is through two angled doors at
each end. The centre panel is inscribed on the
back *Baccio Cappelli Fecit anno 1709
Fiorenza*. The capitals of the columns are of
the type Adam had seen at Spalato and
illustrated in the *Ruins of the Palace of the
Emperor Diocletian at Spalatro in Dalmatia*,
published in London, 1764. Although no
design for this cabinet has survived, there is at
the Soane Museum (vol. 17, no. 218) a design
for a heavier and more architectural cabinet,
which is dated 1 June 1771 and inscribed,
*Design of a Cabinet for Her Grace The
Duchess of Manchester made to receive Eleven
pieces of Scagliola Landskips, the parts shaded
Yellow shew what may be gilt or done in Brass
[or] in Or Moulu. The plain parts may be
executed in woods of Various kinds*. This design
must have been completely revised by Adam
at some time between 1771 and 1775. The
cabinet was apparently ready by April 1775,
when Boulton and Fothergill proposed sending
the metal mounts for a trial fitting before they
were gilded. Their invoice for these ormolu
mounts, dated October 1775, was for the
surprisingly high figure of £73 11s. (L. Boynton,
'Italian Craft in an English Cabinet', *Country
Life*, vol. CXL, 29 September 1966, p. 768, and
Furniture History, vol. II, 1966, p. 31).

N/5   CANDLESTAND

Pine and mahogany with carved decoration
painted in white on a pale blue ground.
One of a pair.
About 1777.
Height 121.9 cm. (48 in.).
W.36–1946.

Designed by Adam for the Eating Room of 20
St James's Square, London, the house of Sir
Watkin Williams-Wynn, built by Adam
between 1771 and 1774. Of three related
designs at the Soane Museum, two (vol. 6,
nos. 53 and 54) are dated 26 April 1777 and
inscribed for Sir Watkin Williams Wynn. The
third (vol. 6, no. 49), which has neither date
nor inscription, is the closest to the pieces as
executed. The colour was governed by the
general colouring of the room and there is a
repetition of some of the motifs in the other
furniture and on the walls. There were
originally four candlestands in the Eating
Room. The other two, which are smaller and
simpler, and without sphinxes, are now in the
Melbourne Art Gallery, Australia.

N/6

N/6 CANDLESTAND
Gilded wood.
One of a pair.
About 1775.
Height 172 cm. (67¾ in.).
W.72–1923.

From the collection of Lord Brownlow at
Belton House, Lincolnshire.

These are designed in the tripod form
favoured by Adam and include in their design
the characteristic rams' heads with swags of
husks (cf. F/3). The clumsiness of certain
parts of the design, however, such as the lower
section of the tripod supports, suggest that
Adam was not responsible for it.

N/7   CANDLESTAND
Gilded pine and composition.
About 1775.
Height 138.8 cm. (54½ in.).
W.37–1937.

In the style of Robert Adam, this candlestand
was perhaps inspired by the pair in the
Drawing Room at Osterley Park (F/3),
although the Osterley ones are far more
elaborate and of a very much higher quality.
There is a hole under each corner of the base,
where peg feet were presumably fitted.

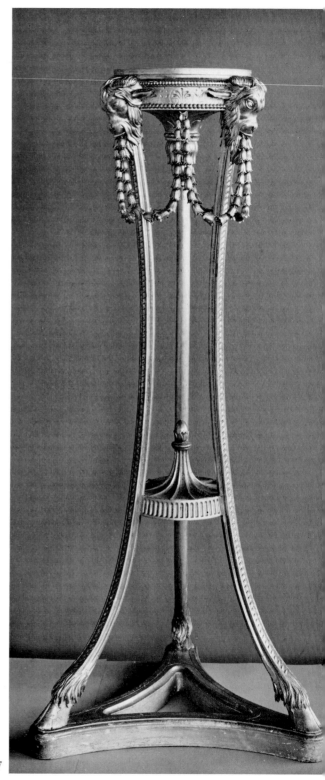

N/7

N/8 SIDE-TABLE
Painted and gilded pine, with painted copper
top.
One of a pair.
About 1780.
Height 81 cm. (32 in.).
349–1871.

These tables are of semi-oval form. The
decoration of the tops, painted on a pink
ground, includes medallions depicting female
figures, which were probably painted by
Angelica Kauffmann.

These tables derive their inspiration from
Adam's marble-topped side-tables, such as that
in the Tapestry Room at Osterley Park (G/4),
but instead of inlaid marble the tops are of
painted copper and the frieze and legs are very
much simplified. In spite of this, the painted
and gilded decoration give them a sumptuous
appearance.

A number of other pieces of furniture of the
period have been found to have their painted
decoration executed on a copper plate. The
technique has the great disadvantage that the
metal expands and contracts under changes of
temperature and this usually causes the paint
to flake off. As a result the painted decoration
of such furniture is usually heavily restored.
In some cases it has been entirely re-painted.

N/8

N/9   ARMCHAIR
Gilded wood; the upholstery, modern.
About 1775.
Height 104 cm. (41 in.).
Given by the Ministry of Works.
W.42–1946.

This armchair, which is similar to a design by
John Linnell in the Department of Prints and
Drawings (E.78–1929), shows marked French
influence in its conception and is a particularly
elegant specimen of the chairmaker's art.

N/10 CABINET

Mahogany, inlaid with satinwood; ebonized
moulding.
About 1775.
Height 215.5 cm. (84¾ in.).
Bequeathed by Sir Herbert Mitchell.
W.50–1936.

The upper stage of this cabinet is based on a
design by John Linnell in the Department of
Prints and Drawings (E.291–1929; pl. N/10a),
although in the drawing the cabinet is
surmounted by a shell motif. The urn-shaped
finial that now surmounts the cabinet was
made in the Museum's Department of
Conservation to replace the marble head of a
Roman Emperor, which was not original. A
similar Linnell design (E.298–1929) does in
fact have a small plinth at the top, like this
cabinet, which is surmounted by a Classical
urn.

A number of Linnell's designs show a similar
serpentine cornice in which the tops of the
doors follow the undulations. It is, in fact, a
very much flattened and simplified Neo-
Classical version of the Baroque broken-scroll
pediment.

The small clasping acanthus leaves on the
doors of both stages are particularly well
carved. The very attractive grain of the
mahogany veneer is also a notable feature of
the cabinet, while the inlaid decoration may be
compared with that on other pieces attributed
to Linnell.

The cavetto section surmounting the lower
stage contains a drawer with a lock. There is an
ebonized moulding above and below it.

Inside the slightly serpentine doors of the base
there are six short drawers and one long one,
all straight-fronted and fitted with handles like
those on the frieze drawer.

Another cabinet based on the same Linnell
design (E.291–1929) was exhibited at the
Antique Dealers' Fair in 1966. This
incorporated the surmounting shell motif as
shown in the drawing.

N/11 CLOCK on PLINTH

The clock of marble with ormolu mounts and
figures of Derby porcelain; the plinth
veneered with satinwood and mahogany, with
a panel painted in brown monochrome.
En suite with barometer N/12.
Dated 1787.
Height 173 cm. (68 in.).
W.15–1958.

The clock movement is contained within the
fluted marble half column, on the ormolu base
of which is engraved *Vulliamy London 1787*.
On the steps leading up to the column are two
books, a sculptor's mallet and a scroll,
inscribed *Fugit irreparabile tempus. Virgil*.

The painted medallion on the plinth shows
Apollo drawing the Chariot of the Sun,
surrounded by signs of the Zodiac.

There is a table clock of similar design at
Buckingham Palace and another pedestal clock
of the same type.

At Syon House there is a clock of very similar
design to the barometer N/12, standing on a
plinth of the same shape but veneered with
scagliola and containing a musical box.

Such clocks were probably all fitted with
protective glass domes.

N/12 BAROMETER on PLINTH

The barometer of marble with ormolu mounts
and figures of Derby porcelain; the plinth
veneered with satinwood and mahogany,
with a panel painted in brown monochrome.
En suite with clock N/11.
About 1787.
Height 173 cm. (68 in.).
W.16–1958.

The dial of the barometer is formed as an
armillary sphere. The front and left-hand sides
of its pedestal are set with Wedgwood plaques
of Diana in her Chariot and Bellerophon with
Pegasus, respectively. On the marble base are
a sextant, a telescope, books and scrolls. The
ormolu base is inscribed *Vulliamy London*.

The painted medallion on the plinth shows
Diana in her Chariot, with a flying cupid
holding the reins and a river god in the
foreground.

The figure of Astronomy with her orrery and a
cupid holding a sextant is similar to that on a
clock at Syon House, made in 1785. The plinth
of the Syon clock is of the same shape as that of
N/12 but veneered with scagliola. It contains a
musical box.

N/13

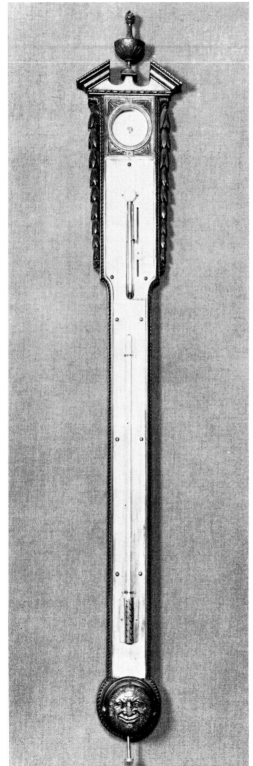

N/13 BAROMETER AND THERMOMETER
Mahogany case.
Third quarter of the 18th century.
Height 122 cm. (48 in.).
Given by Brigadier W. E. Clark, C. M. G.,
D. S. O., D. L., through the National Art-
Collections Fund.
W.17–1957.

The instrument is signed *H. Pyefinch, London*.
Henry Pyefinch (fl. 1739–90), was a well-
known London optical and mathematical
instrument maker, who had premises at
67 Cornhill.

At the top is a wheel-barometer dial. The
mercury reservoir at the base is covered by a
mahogany boss carved in the form of a sun
with a human face. (Some of the decoration,
such as the surmounting urn finial and the low
relief carving round the dial, appears to be of
later date.) (N. Goodison, *English barometers,
1680–1860*, London, 1969, pp. 184–85.)

N/14 MIRROR
Wood, covered with papier-mâché, and gilded.
About 1770.
Height 234 cm. (92 in.).
W.25–1926.

This mirror shows the use of papier-mâché for
intricate ornamental details. Sconces and
candlesticks were already being made of
papier-mâché in France during the
seventeenth century. It was a quick and cheap
substitute for carving and the carvers naturally
tried to resist its introduction into this
country. Even so, by the middle of the
eighteenth century, ornamental details were
being modelled in high relief by this method.
The principal practitioners of this craft were
Frenchmen. The papier-mâché could be
mounted on a wire core when objects in full
relief, such as candlestands, were being made.

N/15 MIRROR
Carved and gilded wood.
About 1785.
Height 234 cm. (92 in.).
W.1–1951.

This mirror still retains a certain amount of
Rococo feeling in its broken outline and
asymmetrical central motifs at top and bottom.
The basically restrained and regular form,
however, particularly of the oval gadrooned
moulding, and the symmetrical arrangement
of the foliage, fruit and flowers are all Neo-
Classical characteristics.

The design would seem to be incomplete, as the
fronds presumably crossed over at the bottom.

N/14

N/15

N/16 WALL-LIGHT
Pine, wire and composition, gilded (the
gilding, modern).
One of a pair.
In the style of about 1790.
Height 62 cm. (24½ in.).
Bequeathed by Mr Edward Hudson through
Messrs Hurford and Taylor.
W.20–1937.

These wall-lights are described in R. E.,
'The Edward and Henry Hudson Bequest to
the Victoria and Albert Museum', *Country
Life*, vol. LXXXI, 10 April 1937, p. 384, and are
also illustrated in *MacQuoid and Edwards*,
vol. III, p. 54, fig. 26.

N/17 ARMCHAIR
Mahogany; upholstered in needlework of
coloured wools.
One of a set of 6.
About 1775.
Height 88 cm. (34½ in.).
Given by F. H. Read Esq.
W.61–1953.

These chairs are almost identical to the set in
the Breakfast Room at Osterley Park, which
are thought to have been designed and made
by John Linnell (K/3). There is, however, no
reason to believe that they came from that
house. The chief differences in the design are
the omission of the fluting on the seat-rail and
the paterae at the leg-joints of the Osterley
chairs but there are also minor differences in
the carving, as, for example, at the junction of
the splat and top-rail.

The general appearance and quality of the
carving suggest that these chairs may also have
been made in the workshop of John Linnell.

N/16

N/17

GROUP O

The furniture of David Garrick

This group of furniture was formerly in the possession of David Garrick, the actor, and came from his villa at Hampton, Middlesex. It is probably part of the painted furniture that Chippendale is known to have supplied to Garrick in about 1770. It may be compared with painted furniture that Chippendale made for the Chinese Bedroom at Nostell Priory, Yorkshire; this is also decorated with a mixture of Neo-Classical and Chinoiserie motifs.

The items from Garrick's bedroom were acquired through the generosity of Mr H. E. Trevor, with the co-operation of some admirers of David Garrick.

(Catalogue of the Sale of Garrick's Villa, 23 June 1864 (*Left-Hand Back Bed Chamber*). For an account of Garrick's villa, see E. Walford, *Greater London*, p. 136.)

O/1 PRESS-BED
Pine, with details painted in dark green on a
white ground; panels of looking-glass; brass
handles.
About 1770.
Height 253 cm. (99½ in.).
W.21–1917.

Unlike the other items in this group this piece
came from the Blue Bedchamber at Garrick's
villa. It is decorated in a purely Neo-
Classical style, with no Chinoiserie, and was
originally blue and white. Although designed
to look like a wardrobe, this piece is actually
a press-bed (a bed made to fold away in a
cupboard or press). At a later date the bed-
fittings were removed and it was in fact
converted into a wardrobe, drawers and
clothes-pegs being fitted in the interior.

The two doors are embellished with decorative
panels of looking-glass, their lower parts
being in the form of sham drawer fronts.

O/1

O/2 WARDROBE
Pine, with details painted in dark green on a
white ground; brass handles.
One of a pair.
About 1770.
Height 167.5 cm. (66 in.).
W.22–1917.

The plain shape and the mouldings are in the
Neo-Classical taste and the Chinoiserie panels
are set in a framework of Neo-Classical form,
with paterae at the corners. O/2 is painted
on one side only, while its pair is completely
plain on both sides. This suggests that one
was designed to stand in a recess and one in
a corner.

Though designed as a pair, the two wardrobes
are quite different. The one illustrated has
two doors, the right-hand compartment
containing shelves and the left, only
extending halfway back, being fitted with
clothes-pegs. Behind this there is a compartment, reached by a door in the side of
the wardrobe, containing deep drawers and a
secret drawer.

The companion wardrobe is divided
horizontally into two parts, with four doors,
the whole of the interior being fitted with
runners for movable shelves.

O/3 CORNER CUPBOARD
Pine, with details painted in dark green on a
white ground.
About 1770.
Height 96.5 cm. (38 in.).
W.24–1917.

As with the wardrobe (O/2), the panels of
Chinoiserie are combined with Neo-Classical
decoration, in this case on the legs and stiles.

There is a single shelf inside.

O/3

O/2

O/4

O/4   CHAIR
Beech, painted to simulate bamboo, with dark
green spots on a white ground; the rush seat
painted white with green stripes.
One of a set of 5.
About 1770.
Height 91.5 cm. (36 in.).
W.25–1917.

These chairs, though not of Neo-Classical
design, form part of the bedroom suite.

O/5

O/5   BASIN STAND
Beech, with details painted in dark green on a white ground.
Of uncertain date.
Height 96.5 cm. (38 in.).
W.31–1917.

This basin stand has been included because it long formed part of the same group of bedroom furniture, although its appearance hardly suggests that it was made in the eighteenth century; moreover, the only detail of the decoration that could be construed as Neo-Classical is the patera on the shelf. The scrolling foliage on the back bears some relationship to that on the wardrobes and the spots recall the similar decoration on the chairs, though there is no attempt to simulate bamboo in this case. It was presumably made about 1830 to go with the rest of the Garrick furniture.

O/6   TOWEL HORSE
Beech, painted with dark green spots on a white ground.
About 1770.
Height 93 cm. (36⅝ in.).
W.32–1917.

This is decorated in a similar manner to the wash-stand but probably belongs to the original suite.

O/7 BEDSTEAD
Beech and pine, painted in dark green on a
white ground; hangings of Indian painted
cotton.
About 1770.
Height 244 cm. (96 in.).
W.70–1916.

This bedstead was also made for Garrick's
Hampton villa. It had been slightly reduced in
height and width before its acquisition by the
Museum in order to fit into the bedroom of a
former owner. The painted hangings were
produced at Masulipatam, Madras, to the
order of the East India Company. Garrick
reported that his wife had trouble with the
customs when bringing them into the
country.

O/7

O/8   HALL CHAIR
Birch, painted with green decoration on a
white ground.
One of a pair.
About 1775.
Height 98 cm. (38½ in.).
W.32–1937.

Like the foregoing suite of bedroom furniture,
these chairs formed part of the furnishing of
David Garrick's villa at Hampton, Middlesex,
and were probably also supplied by
Chippendale.

O/8

GROUP P

Chairs with shield-, oval-, and heart-shaped backs

This group consists of chairs, all of which have backs of shield-, oval-, or heart-shape, of the type generally known as 'Hepplewhite'. In fact none of them is actually reflected in a Hepplewhite design but the motifs of which the openwork splats are formed, such as urns, swags of drapery, paterae and the Prince of Wales's feathers can be seen in similar combinations in *Hepplewhite*.

During this period the best chairs were designed and made without stretchers and, where these are present, it is likely that the chair is of provincial origin.

P/1   ARMCHAIR
Mahogany.
About 1776.
Height 99 cm. (39 in.).
Given by Commander Walter N. Westhead,
R. N. V. R.
W.2–1946.

One of a set of 9 chairs, of which the rest are in
the possession of the donor.

The set of nine chairs, including two armchairs,
was acquired by Jonathan Pytts for his house
at Kyre Park, Worcestershire, in about 1776.
One of these, still with its original leather-
covered seat is illustrated by H. A. Tipping in
English homes, vol. VI, pt. 1, London, 1926,
fig. 124.

P/2   ARMCHAIR
Mahogany; upholstered in brown horse-hair.
About 1780.
Height 93.5 cm. (36¾ in.).
725–1897.

P/2

P/1

P/3

P/3   CHAIR
Mahogany.
About 1780.
One of a pair.
Height 95.5 cm. (37½ in.).
Bequeathed by Miss Amy E. Tomes.
W.70–1940.

P/4   ARMCHAIR
Mahogany, inlaid with satinwood.
About 1780.
Height 98 cm. (38½ in.).
1458–1904.

Hepplewhite illustrates the use of the Prince of
Wales's feathers combined with an oval back
in plate 8 of the *Guide*, 1st ed., 1788.

P/4

P/5

P/6

P/5 ARMCHAIR
Mahogany; the upholstery, modern.
About 1780.
Height 96.5 cm. (38 in.).
Bequeathed by Claude Rotch Esq.
W.27–1962.

This armchair is stamped with the letters
'H. I.' under the seat-rail.

Heart-shaped backs, popular at the same time
as those of oval- or shield-shape, were decorated
with similar carving. The central part of this
design, incorporating drapery swags and the
Prince of Wales's feathers, is the same as that
on the foregoing armchair (P/4). An armchair
and a side-chair having backs of the same
design as this are illustrated in the records for
1788 of Gillow and Sons.

P/6 ARMCHAIR
Mahogany; upholstered in reddish-brown
horse-hair.
About 1785(?).
En suite with a side-chair.
Height 96.5 cm. (38 in.).
Given by Eric M. Browett Esq.
W.68–1937.

The Prince of Wales's feathers are confined
within the hoop-like member in an awkward
manner and the chairs are rather heavy. It is
possible that they may be nineteenth-century
reproductions.

P/7

P/7 ARMCHAIR
Satinwood, painted in various colours; cane seat.
One of 4, probably all from the same set of 18.
About 1790.
Height 93 cm. (36½ in.).
This chair, with two others, given by Mrs A. E. Ingham; the fourth chair (W.59–1936) given by Mrs Simon Green.
W.1–1968.

This chair is part of a set of eighteen chairs supplied by Seddon, Sons and Shackleton to D. Tupper of Hauteville House, Guernsey, in about 1790. The original bill, headed 'George Seddon & Sons, J. Shackleton', reads *18 Satinwood Elbow Chairs round fronts & hollow can'd seats neatly Japanned— ornamented with roses in back and peacock feather border @ 73/6 ea. £66. 3. 0.*

All the chairs are stamped under the back seat-rail, two with the letters 'W. R.' and two with 'I. P.' A pair of chairs that was in the Swaythling Collection in 1965 is similarly stamped 'I. P.'

P/8

P/8 ARMCHAIR
Satinwood, painted in various colours; cane seat.
About 1887. Stamped 4736.
Height 97 cm. (38¼ in.).
240–1887.

This chair was made in about 1887 by Messrs Wright and Mansfield of New Bond Street, London, probably having been purchased directly from them as an example of contemporary design. The firm played a considerable part in bringing about a revival of interest in late eighteenth-century English furniture, not least by exhibiting a high quality satinwood cabinet in the Adam style at the Paris Exhibition of 1867.

This chair closely resembles the previous example, differing only slightly in the form and the painted details.

P/9

P/10   ARMCHAIR
Painted brown and partly gilded; the
upholstery, 19th century.
One of a set of 5.
About 1780.
Height 93.5 cm. (36¾ in.).
H.H.148–1948.

This armchair forms part of the contents of
Ham House. A number of chairs having oval
backs filled with a large anthemion motif were
made at about this time, although Hepplewhite
does not illustrate the type in the *Guide*. Such
a chair is illustrated on the trade-card of
Vickers and Rutledge of Conduit Street,
London (the firm was active between about
1775 and 1780; see A. Heal, *London
furniture makers*, London, 1953, pp. 182 and
189). There is also a design for a chair of this
type in the records of Gillow and Sons, dated
March 1785.

There is a set of similar chairs at Houghton
Hall, Norfolk.

P/9   ARMCHAIR
Beech, painted in various colours on a light
brown ground. (The paint is now much worn.)
About 1790.
Height 95 cm. (37½ in.).
W.90–1911.

This chair may be compared with P/7, in
which the ornament is painted on satinwood.

In the introduction to the *Guide*, 3rd ed., 1794,
Hepplewhite says, 'For chairs, a new and very
elegant fashion has arisen within these few
years, of finishing them with painted or
japanned work, which gives a rich and
splendid appearance to the minuter parts of the
ornaments, which are generally thrown in by
the painter. Several of these designs are
particularly adapted to this style, which allows
a frame-work less massy than is requisite for
mahogany; and by assorting the prevailing
colour to the furniture and light of the room,
affords opportunity, by the variety of grounds
which may be introduced, to make the whole
in harmony, with a pleasing and striking
effect to the eye. Japanned chairs should have
cane bottoms, with linen or cotton cases over
cushions to accord with the general hue of the
chair.'

P/10

P/11

P/12

P/11 CHAIR
Mahogany, inlaid with a panel of painted
satinwood; the upholstery, modern.
About 1785.
Height 95 cm. (37½ in.).
510–1907.

The pierced splat in this chair, which clearly
shows its derivation from the mid-century type
used by Chippendale, is embellished with the
Neo-Classical motifs of an urn with rams'
heads and a small panel painted with a patera
and husks.

The modern upholstery detracts from the
elegant appearance of the chair.

P/12 CHAIR
Mahogany; the upholstery modern.
About 1785.
Height 94 cm. (37 in.).
W.68–1935.

The modern upholstery is rather too thick and
should probably have a double row of gilt
nails, which would give the whole seat a lighter
appearance.

The letters 'I. D.' are stamped underneath the
back seat-rail.

P/13

P/13   ARMCHAIR

Beech, painted an ivory colour, with decoration in various colours, some on a black ground; the upholstery, modern.
About 1785.
Height 94 cm. (37 in.).
W.52–1946.

The design of this chair is not entirely happy as the back is rather small for the seat and arms. Moreover, the latter are joined to the back in a somewhat awkward manner (cf. P/4). In many chairs of this type a painted panel fills the whole of the oval that is, in this example, occupied by the web-like feature.

The seat-rail has been restored.

P/14   ARMCHAIR

Mahogany; the upholstery, modern.
About 1780.
Height 96.5 cm. (38 in.).
269–1908.

This chair shows the retention of certain Rococo features, notably the cabriole legs, terminating in 'French' scroll feet. A chair with legs of similar type is illustrated in *Hepplewhite*, 1st ed., 1788, pl. 12.

P/14

P/15 ARMCHAIR

Beech and mahogany, painted brown;
upholstered in red, black and brown woollen
embroidery.
About 1780.
Height 90 cm. (35½ in.).
W.36–1919.

In this chair the shield-shape is adopted for an
upholstered back. There is a somewhat similar
design in *Hepplewhite*, 1st ed., 1788, pl. 10e,
which also has baluster legs, of a slightly
different type, but in which the shield-back
does not have such pronounced corners. This
type of armchair, having an upholstered back,
is called a 'cabriole' chair by Hepplewhite,
although he also includes under this heading
one example which has an openwork back
(pl. 11).

The needlework is probably original, in which
case it is a rare survivor, since materials of this
type, with such comparatively simple patterns,
have not often been thought worthy of
preservation once they have become worn.
However, it was precisely patterns such as this
which were in favour during the later decades
of the eighteenth century for upholstery
purposes. Stripes—so often associated with the
Regency—were in fact also very popular
during the same period.

P/15

GROUP Q

Chairs with variously shaped backs

This group of furniture comprises chairs with backs of various types, ranging from those that still retain some characteristics of the Rococo style to several examples of the square-backed type that largely replaced the curvilinear shapes towards the end of the century.

Several items have overall painted decoration, known at that time as 'japanning'. Painted decoration, generally carried out on beech, became popular in the second half of the eighteenth century and was considerably cheaper to execute than carving or marquetry which required the use of more expensive wood and was of course more laborious. The term 'japanning' did not necessarily refer to the imitation of Oriental lacquer, as it does today. Indeed, such chinoiserie was little favoured at that time.

Q/1   ARMCHAIR
Mahogany; the upholstery, modern.
About 1775.
Height 91.5 cm. (36 in.).
Given by Edward Dent Esq.
W.21–1922.

The serpentine outlines of back- and seat-rail
and the cabriole legs are derived from the
Rococo style, although the restrained curves of
the latter and the fluting would not have been
used at an earlier period. The arcading of
pointed arches in the back is in the 'Gothick
Taste' but these, like the seat-rail, are
punctuated with Neo-Classical paterae.

Q/2   ARMCHAIR
Mahogany; the upholstery, modern.
About 1780.
Height 97 cm. (38¼ in.).
503–1907.

The arms terminate in a ball or fruit partially
enclosed in leaves, a motif favoured by John
Linnell (cf. the armchair from the Breakfast
Room at Osterley Park, K/3), but the carving
on this chair is not of the high quality usually
found in Linnell's work. The simple treatment
of the legs and the use of stretchers also
suggest a provincial maker.

The badly padded upholstery spoils the dished
line of the seat.

Q/1

Q/2

Q/3   CHAIR
Mahogany; the upholstery, modern.
One of a set of 4.
About 1785.
Height 94 cm. (37 in.).
Bequeathed by Miss Amy E. Tomes.
W.77–1940.

The shape of the back is rather similar to that
of the foregoing armchair (Q/2), but it is a far
less accomplished design.

The initials 'R. S.', presumably those of the
maker, are stamped under the back of the seat
frame.

Q/4   CHAIR
Mahogany; upholstered in pink silk brocade.
Of uncertain date.
Height 96 cm. (37¾ in.).
W.66–1937.

The design of this chair, although it
incorporates such Neo-Classical motifs as the
anthemion and strings of husks and bell-
flowers, still owes a lot to the mid-century
style of Chippendale. The splat is divided with
openings headed by Gothic arches and the
carved ribbon decoration is strongly
reminiscent of Chippendale's 'ribband-back'
designs. The splat is not fitted into a 'shoe' in
the normal eighteenth-century manner and
there are pegged joints of a curious nature
in the front seat-rail. These facts, together with
the incompatibility of the delicate carving
in the back with the very rugged legs suggests
that the chair has been altered at some stage.

Q/3

Q/4

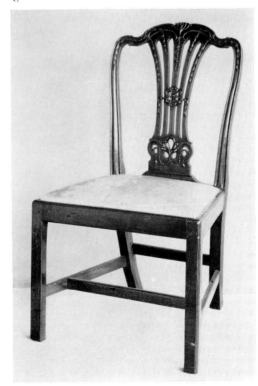

Q/5 ARMCHAIR
Beech, painted brown; red canvas upholstery.
About 1775.
Height 93 cm. (36½ in.).
W.452–1922.

This armchair displays an unusual mixture of
styles. The rounded back and curved, fluted
seat-rail, as well as the delicately-shaped arms,
are all forms associated with the Neo-Classical
style. On the other hand, the openwork
carving of the back, incorporating pointed
arches, suggests the 'Gothick Taste', as do the
legs, carved in the form of cluster-columns.

Q/6 ARMCHAIR
Mahogany; upholstered in green leather.
About 1780.
Height 91 cm. (35¾ in.).
Bequeathed by John Murray Elger, through
Messrs Ellis Peirs and Co.
W.8–1955.

Q/5

Q/6

Q/7   ARMCHAIR
Mahogany; the upholstery, modern.
About 1785.
Height 96 cm. (37¾ in.).
Given by Eric M. Browett Esq.
W.67–1957.

The tri-partite splat, in which each upright is
headed by stylized leaves, became fashionable
about 1785. *Hepplewhite*, 1st ed., 1788,
illustrates, pl. 2d, a design for a shield-back
chair incorporating similar forms.

The upholstery is now too thick and spoils the
dished line of the seat.

Q/8   CHAIR
Mahogany; upholstered in brown leather.
Dated 1783.
Height 88.5 cm. (34¾ in.).
Bequeathed by Miss Amy E. Tomes.
W.47–1940.

The chair is inscribed in ink on the underside
of the front seat-rail *Samuel Fairhead/
August 1783*. This is probably the name of the
original owner. There is a serial number
XXXXVII, stamped four times, one on each of the
inner sides of the seat frame. (The urn table,
S/8, is another example of a piece inscribed
with the name of an owner or maker.)
This is an early example of the square-backed
type of chair that replaced the oval and other
curvilinear shapes in popularity towards the
end of the century.

Q/7

Q/8

Q/9 CHAIR
Mahogany; the upholstery modern.
About 1785.
Height 89.5 cm. (35¼ in.).
Given by Eric M. Browett Esq.
W.70–1937.

The back of this chair, incorporating an
elongated vase-form together with the Prince
of Wales's feathers, closely resembles plate 1 in
Hepplewhite, 3rd ed., 1794. It does not appear
in the first edition of 1788 and Hepplewhite
seems to have copied the square-back from
Sheraton, who had commented adversely on
Hepplewhite's earlier chair-designs (R.
Fastnedge, *Sheraton furniture*, London, 1962,
p. 49).

Q/10 CHAIR
Mahogany; the upholstery modern.
One of a set of 4.
About 1785.
Height 91.5 cm. (36 in.).
Bequeathed by Miss Amy E. Tomes.
W.81–1940.

The upholstery is too thickly padded and
destroys the lines of this otherwise very
graceful chair.

Q/9

Q/10

Q/11 ARMCHAIR
Mahogany; the upholstery, modern.
About 1790.
Height 92.5 cm. (36½ in.).
W.48–1927.

The form of the splats resembles those on the painted armchair at Osterley Park (Q/15) of about the same date.

Q/12 ARMCHAIR
Beech, painted chocolate brown, with white lines and decoration in various colours; cane seat.
One of a pair.
About 1790.
Height 93.5 cm. (36¾ in.).
Given by Richard Crossley Sharman Esq.
W.4–1941.

The back combines the elongated vase-form often used with this type of openwork splat (cf. Q/9), with naturalistically painted flowers on a solid background. Chair-backs with a raised centre-section to the top-rail are illustrated in *Hepplewhite*, 1st ed., 1788, pls. 6 and 11. There are several examples of chairs having this feature in *Sheraton*, pls. 32–6.

Q/11

Q/12

Q/13   ARMCHAIR

Mahogany; the upholstery, modern.
About 1785.
Height 87.5 cm. ($34\frac{1}{2}$ in.).
Given by Donald Gunn Esq.
W.64–1930.

This armchair, with its square, padded back
and padded sides, is strongly influenced by
French chairs of the period, though the legs are
somewhat longer than they would have been
on contemporary French examples. The
upward curve of the arms to join the back near
the top was a feature that was to be widely
adopted in England in subsequent years.

Q/13

Q/14   ARMCHAIR

Mahogany, with brass rods in the arms and
back; the upholstery, modern (some of the
brass rods are recent replacements).
About 1790.
Height 87.6 cm. ($34\frac{1}{2}$ in.).
45–1869.

This chair is noteworthy in that the top-rail of
the back fits *between* the uprights in the French
manner. The Classical lyre, used by both
Robert Adam and John Linnell for chair-backs,
had also been adopted by certain French
designers—notably Georges Jacob—and this
armchair may well have been made under the
influence of François Hervé, the émigré
chairmaker, who worked for Henry Holland
and for the Prince Regent at Carlton House.
Hervé also produced chairs with backs
constructed in this way for Lady Spencer at
Althorp in 1791.

Q/14

Q/15

Q/15 ARMCHAIR
Beech, painted in various colours on a white ground; cane seat, with a leather squab cushion.
One of a set of 6. *En suite* with 6 side-chairs (Q/16).
About 1790.
Height 89.5 cm. (35¼ in.).
O.P.H.216–1949.

This set of 6 armchairs forms part of the contents of Osterley Park and was perhaps originally made for one of the garden buildings at Osterley.

Q/16

Q/16 CHAIR
Beech, painted in various colours on a white ground; cane seat.
One of a set of 6. *En suite* with 6 armchairs (Q/15).
About 1790.
Height 86 cm. (33¾ in.).
O.P.H.222–1949.

Like the armchairs, Q/15, these chairs were probably made for a garden building at Osterley.

Q/17   CHAIR

Painted beech and cane. (The original colours
appear to have been green and white but some
have been repainted in other colours.)
One of a set of 19.
About 1775.
Height 87.5 cm. ($34\frac{1}{2}$ in.).
O.P.H.334–1949.

These chairs, forming part of the contents of
Osterley Park, are not definitely identifiable in
the inventory of 1782 but they may perhaps be
survivors from the original *Twenty four green
and white Cabriole Chairs cane seats and backs
Cushions covered with mixt Damask and Check
Cases* that were in the Long Gallery at the
time the inventory was made. The term
'Cabriole' was not, of course, being used to
refer to the shape of the legs but neither was it
necessarily used in the same sense as by
Hepplewhite, who says, in the *Guide*, 'Chairs
with stuffed backs are called cabriole chairs'.

The design is not typical of Adam's work. The
back is in a cartouche shape and is constructed
in a manner more typical of French, than of
English, chairs, with the top-rail of the back
fitted between, instead of on top of, the
uprights. Indeed, this shape of back was more
favoured in France than in England.

There is a design among the Linnell drawings
in the Victoria and Albert Museum for a chair
of slightly earlier style, having cabriole legs,
which also has a cane panel in the back and is
similarly painted in green and white
(illustrated in H. Hayward, 'The Drawings of
John Linnell in the Victoria and Albert
Museum', *Furniture History*, vol. v, 1969,
fig. 6).

Squab cushions, with which the seats would
originally have been fitted, would reduce the
size of the gap below the back.

Q/17

Q/18

Q/18 MUSIC STOOL

Beech and oak, painted with pale blue
decoration on a white ground; cane back panel;
leather upholstery.
Of uncertain date.
Height 87.5 cm. (34½ in.).
O.P.H.24–1949.

This music stool forms part of the contents of
Osterley Park. It is not mentioned in the
inventory of 1782 and it was probably made
early in the nineteenth century with vaguely
Adamesque features to fit in with the
surroundings. There is a small square pianoforte, dated 1773, and made by the London
maker, Johannes Pohlman, at Osterley (Y/2),
for which this music stool may have been made.
However, illustrations suggest that people did
not use specially designed seat-furniture for
playing keyboard instruments in the
eighteenth century. An early record of a
'Round Music Stool' is given, however, in *The
Prices of Cabinet Work*, 1797. This was
described as 'Thirteen inches diameter, to
rise with a screw, the top fram'd, veneer'd,
and a bead under ditto; on four plain
Marlboro' legs, and a fram'd stretcher'
(J. Gloag, *A short dictionary of furniture*,
London, 1969).

A music stool having very similar construction
and design, except for the back, was lent from
Claydon House, Buckinghamshire, to the Loan
Exhibition of English Furniture at the Bethnal
Green Museum in 1896. (The design of the
back suggests a date of about 1820.) A music
stool of similar construction but without a back
is illustrated in the records of Gillow and Sons
and is dated 1825. There is a photographic
record of a music stool with a lyre-back of
Regency type, which has similarly shaped legs,
seat and underframing to the Osterley one
and an example of this type was in the London
market in 1969.

GROUP R

Seat furniture, other than chairs

This group consists of seat furniture, other than chairs.

R/1 STOOL
Mahogany.
About 1765.
Height 50.2 cm. (19¾ in.).
Given by Brigadier W. E. Clark, C.M.G., D.S.O.,
D.L., through the National Art-Collections Fund.
W.5–1963.

There is a late nineteenth-century label under
the seat, bearing the printed inscription, *To
H. S. H. The Prince & Princess of Teck |
John Lane 47 Sloane Street S. W. | Carver and
Gilder | Dealers in antique china, furniture &
works of art.*

R/2 WINDOW SEAT
Beech and mahogany, painted in various
colours on a dark brown ground.
Late 18th century.
Height 66 cm. (26 in.).
Given by Mrs Walter W. Parish.
W.29–1926.

This was clearly made to fit into a tapering
recess—possibly a window-bay. Stools were
placed in the window-bays in many rooms
furnished under the guidance of Robert Adam.

Part of the original printed cotton cover can be
seen under the later upholstery.

R/3 WINDOW SEAT
Beech, painted white, with ornament in blue
on a gilt ground.
Late 18th century.
Height 71 cm. (28 in.).
Given by Mrs Dora Hedges.
W.39–1953.

This form was much favoured by Robert Adam
and no doubt his example was followed by
many other English architects and decorators,
who would have ordered such 'scroll-headed'
stools for rather humbler homes they were
doing up.

R/2

R/3

R/4   SETTEE
Painted in various colours on a black ground;
cane panels in the back and sides; webbing seat
with a squab cushion; brass castors.
About 1790.
Height 94.5 cm. (37¼ in.).
W.41–1931.

This is essentially an extended version of a
common form of late eighteenth-century
English chair. The inset balusters forming the
uprights to the arms are of French derivation.

A sofa of similar design to this is illustrated in
the records of Gillow and Sons for 1794, where
the back is stated to have had '3 loose
Cushions'; no doubt this sofa also originally
had loose cushions for the back.

R/4

GROUP S

Tables and Stands

This group contains tables and stands of various kinds, including four examples of the so-called 'Pembroke' table, a new form, based on the mid-eighteenth-century 'breakfast table', which first appeared at this period.

As with the chairs in Group Q, three kinds of decoration are exemplified: carving, marquetry-work and painting.

S/1   PEMBROKE TABLE
Satinwood, with marquetry of various woods.
Leather castors.
About 1780.
Height 73.5 cm. (29 in.).
Given by Gerald Kerin Ltd.
W.6–1959.

A table of this type is illustrated in
Hepplewhite, pl. 62.

Sheraton describes a Pembroke table in the
Cabinet Dictionary, 1803, as 'a kind of
breakfast table, from the name of the lady who
first gave orders for one of them'. The term
is used for a small, lightly-constructed table,
having two flaps, supported by hinged wooden
brackets; the frieze usually contains a drawer
or drawers. It differs from a breakfast table in
that the latter normally has a shelf enclosed by
fretted sides and a pair of doors.

S/2   PEMBROKE TABLE
Satinwood veneer, cross-banded with
mahogany and decorated with marquetry of
various woods, some stained green. Leather
castors.
About 1780.
Height 72 cm. (28¼ in.).
Bequeathed by Claude Rotch Esq.
W.28–1962.

Of a similar type to S/1, except that the flaps
are lobed. When extended, they are supported
by pairs of brackets having wooden hinges.
There is a drawer at one end.

S/1

S/2

S/3   PEMBROKE TABLE
Mahogany, inlaid with satinwood and other
woods; brass castors and knobs.
About 1790.
Height 72.5 cm. (28½ in.).
Bequeathed by Mrs C. P. Holliday.
W.8–1935.

S/4   PEMBROKE TABLE
Mahogany, cross-banded with rosewood;
castors and drawer handles of brass.
About 1790.
Height 73.5 cm. (29 in.).
Bequeathed by V. B. Crowther-Beynon Esq.,
through A. Gray Esq.
W.16–1952.

A top of irregular shape such as this was often
favoured for Pembroke tables, as it served to
conceal the frame better than an oval one. The
characteristically slender legs are here braced
by stretchers. These were not a normal feature
and may have been added later: certainly a
stretcher springing from a leg of columnar
form is not entirely satisfactory.

S/3

S/4

S/5   DINING TABLE
Mahogany, inlaid with holly and ebony;
sunken brass castors.
One of a pair.
About 1775.
Height 75 cm. (29½ in.).
W.37–1929.

This type of dining table, which became very
popular in the last quarter of the eighteenth
century, consists of two tables with folding
flaps supported on gate-legs, which can be
fitted together back-to-back to form one large
table. The two sections can serve as side-tables,
with the flaps concealed at the back, when the
table is not in use for dining.

The top has an inlaid border of holly and ebony
in a checker pattern. The brass castors are
recessed in the block feet.

S/6   TEA TABLE
Beech, painted with green decoration on a
white ground; the top, varnished.
About 1790.
Height 72.5 cm. (28½ in.).
O.P.H.239–1949.

This small table forms part of the contents of
Osterley Park and was probably used in one of
the bedrooms on the upper floor or in a garden
building.

S/7   OCCASIONAL TABLE
Beech and oak, painted white; the top
decorated in various colours and varnished.
About 1790.
Height 76 cm. (30 in.).
O.P.H.21–1949.

Like the last example, this small table forms
part of the contents of Osterley Park and was
probably used in one of the bedrooms on the
upper floor or in a garden building.

S/5

S/6

S/7

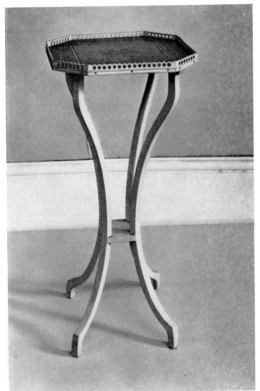

S/8 URN TABLE

Satinwood, with painted decoration in green and whitish-yellow and painted black stringing lines; ivory handles.
About 1790.
Height 72.5 cm. (28½ in.).
Bequeathed by Lady Isabella D. Wilson.
W.45–1935.

The top is of a 'D' shape with a hinged leaf on the straight side. The drop-leaf, which is supported on a hinged bracket, is painted with an oval wreath and the main part of the top with a trophy design. There is a drawer at either end.

Under the flap there is the inscription, in ink, *M. Gregson Liverpool 1790*. This is probably the name of the original owner and suggests that the table, a rare type, may represent the design of a local cabinet-maker at Liverpool.

The splay leg, used on so many pieces of furniture at this time, serves to give greater stability to this very delicate design.

S/8

S/9 SIDE-TABLE
Satinwood, painted in various colours.
One of a pair. (The other is at the Portsmouth
Art Gallery.)
About 1780.
Height 92.5 cm. (36½ in.).
W.5–1966.

The top is decorated with garlands of flowers
centring on a grisaille plaque, showing three
cupids with wreath, bows and arrows. The
central plaque on the frieze depicts an urn,
flanked by heraldic supporters, amidst
acanthus scrolls. Holes along the lower edge of
the frieze suggest that the table may once have
had some form of pendent decoration, such as
carved garlands, between the legs.

Tables of this type were frequently made in
pairs and were used either as pier-tables,
between windows, or as side-tables on any of
the other walls. The semi-circular, or elliptical,
top, made popular by Adam, was particularly
favoured.

S/10 SIDE-TABLE
Pine, veneered with satinwood, burr walnut
and other woods; some decoration in green
paint.
About 1785.
Height 91.5 cm. (36 in.).
325–1878.

The half-oval top is decorated with a fan-
shaped ornament between borders of sprays
and festoons of husks. The decoration on the
fronts of the legs is in green paint.

The slender legs of this piece well illustrate the
extreme attenuation of much furniture made
during the last two decades of the eighteenth
century in this country.

S/9

S/10

S/11

S/11 SIDE-TABLE
Pine, painted in various colours on an ivory ground.
About 1790. (Irish.)
Height 92 cm. (36¼ in.).
W.10–1920.

In the centre of the frieze are the arms of Ussher: *azure a chevron ermine between three batons argent*. The crest is *a cubit arm vested azure cuffed argent grasping a baton also argent*.

On the top is an oval panel painted *en grisaille*, portraying a young man seated at a table and writing: it is inscribed *Lucy Ussher Fecit*. Lucy Arabella Ussher (died 1844) was the daughter of John Ussher of Landscape, Co. Wexford.

S/12

S/12   READING STAND
Mahogany; brass handles.
One of a pair.
About 1775.
Height 93.5cm. (36¾ in.).
O.P.H.275–1949.

The cabriole form is retained for the legs of the
tripod in this piece but it is of the
characteristically slender type in use at this
time (cf. V/1).

Hepplewhite, 1st ed., 1788, illustrates two
'Reading Desks' on tripods with cabriole legs
and adjustable tops (pl. 51) but they are also
fitted with a telescopic extension in the
vertical shaft.

GROUP T

Fitted Tables and small Cabinets

This group consists of small tables and cabinets designed for various specialized activities, such as writing, dressing and needlework. A great many compact pieces of this type were made after about 1770, intended mainly for the use of ladies. Some of them contain elaborate and ingenious fittings, very often combining accessories for several occupations in the same piece.

T/1 DRESSING-TABLE

Mahogany; brass handles.
Third quarter of the 18th century.
Height 84.5 cm. (33¼ in.).
Bequeathed by Claude Rotch Esq.
W.41–1962.

This piece is typical of the small dressing-tables that were so common in the second half of the eighteenth century. This type was principally used by men and had a bowl and mirror for shaving.

The top three drawer-fronts are false and mask compartments for a bowl, etc., reached by opening the pair of hinged lids which swing open to form trays suitable for holding the contents of a man's pockets. The dished circle at the crossing of the stretchers is for a water jug. The sliding mirror is missing.

The fretted brackets and the stretcher display a Rococo character, suggesting that this table was not made much after 1770.

T/1

T/2 DRESSING-CASE ON STAND

Satinwood with inlay and veneer of kingwood and other woods; silver mounts; ivory knob handles; brass castors.
About 1780.
Height 89 cm. (35 in.).
Given by Miss Joan D. Parkes.
W.29–1939.

The interior is lined with red leather and red plush. It is fitted with a tray, which is divided into compartments containing: a pair of metal spurs; a silver tube for shaving soap; a pair of cut-glass inkpots with silver covers; a double-ended caustic holder; a double-ended toothbrush; a metal tongue scraper; a pair of tall cut-glass bottles with silver tops; 4 steel razors with decorated backs and tortoiseshell cases; a hone; a razor strop in a case; a large oval silver box with the London hallmark for 1780; a pair of similar small oval silver boxes; a tubular silver container; a pair of tall square cut-glass bottles; a knife, two forks, a spoon and a pair of nail clippers.

The case is pegged on to the stand.

T/2

T/3 DRESSING-TABLE

Mahogany, with marquetry of satinwood, harewood, laburnum, holly and other woods, some stained green; ormolu mounts.
About 1770.
Height 71 cm. (28 in.).
Given by Mrs H. H. Mulliner through
R. Freeman Smith Esq.
W.89–1924.

The marquetry design of the top is composed with a central feature of an oval enclosing a vase and festoons. The front pulls out as a drawer and the top can be pushed back so as to disclose a hinged, adjustable mirror, which is pivoted and has a baize-covered writing surface on the back. The lids of the compartments on either side are inlaid respectively with a portrait of a woman and a man in Oriental costume on the undersides and the same figures, reversed, on the tops. There is a small drawer in the middle of the main drawer, which is released by a wooden spring catch underneath.

The cabriole legs terminate in ormolu-mounted feet and are typical of the very attenuated type used on a great deal of furniture at this period. These, and the serpentine lower edge of the frieze, are vestiges of the Rococo taste. They can be seen, in similar form, in the stand supporting a cabinet (U/12).

T/3

T/4

T/4   DRESSING-TABLE
Satinwood, inlaid with various woods; ivory handles.
About 1785.
Height 109 cm. (43 in.).
W.8–1951.

The central section of the top is hinged at the back and opens to reveal a large shallow compartment. It has a lock in the front frieze. The opening of the central flap releases the two flanking lids, which swing outwards to reveal narrow compartments. There are no drawers, although these are suggested by the ivory handles and stringing lines at the front.

T/5   DRESSING-TABLE
Mahogany, veneered with harewood and inlaid with various woods; brass handles and castors.
About 1780.
Height 76 cm. (30 in.).
Given by Mrs Anna L. Bliss.
W.42–1934.

The top has a central flap opening towards the back, flanked by two that open outwards, all of which have marquetry decoration of floral sprays. Below the central flap there is a hinged leaf, covered with green velvet, which can be raised on a ratchet. Under this is a shallow compartment with a small drawer at the back. Below the side flaps there are trays, divided into compartments, for toilet requisites. The upper two drawer-fronts are false.

T/5

T/6 DRESSING-TABLE
Mahogany, veneered with harewood,
satinwood and tulipwood.
About 1790.
Height 93 cm. (36½ in.).
Given by S. M. Messer Esq.
W.14–1959.

A dressing-table of similar type is illustrated in
the appendix to *Sheraton*, 3rd ed., 1802, pl. xx.

The upper part, containing variously shaped
compartments for toilet requisites, can be
lifted off the stand. It has had a Bramah lock
fitted to it.

The stand contains a brushing slide and two
drawers. The shelf is a later addition.

T/6

T/7   WRITING-TABLE AND DESK
Harewood, inlaid with various woods.
About 1780.
Height 84 cm. (33 in.).
Bequeathed by B. H. Webb Esq.
W.127–1919.

Although the box on top is designed to look as
though it is fitted with two drawers, it is, in
fact, hinged at the front and opens to form a
desk. It has a lock at the back in the same way
as the standard writing-box of the period.

There are two hinged writing-flaps, covered
with green baize, having compartments
below, and at the back two compartments for
ink and pounce pots and a tray for pens.

There is a false drawer in the front frieze, the
real drawer, fitted with a lock, being on the
right-hand side.

The hinges of the writing-box are stamped with
a cursive 'P'.

T/7

T/8

T/8   WRITING- AND WORK-TABLE
AND READING DESK
Satinwood, inlaid with mahogany; brass
handles; green pleated silk panel.
About 1790.
Height 76 cm. (30 in.).
Given by John Garwood Esq. (Frank and
Helen Lloyd Bequest).
W.59–1927.

Below the adjustable top, which can be tilted
to form a reading stand, there is a swivelling
shelf at either side, on which to stand a
candlestick. On the right there is a drawer
fitted with small compartments for writing
materials. A silk work-bag on a wooden frame
can be pulled out at the other side. The frieze
at the front is in the form of a false drawer,
with ring handles. At the back, a fire-screen
with a panel of pleated silk can be drawn up.

T/9 WORK-TABLE

Beech and pine, painted white; applied
ornament of gilded composition; green silk bag.
About 1790.
Height 77 cm. (30¼ in.).
O.P.H.19–1949.

This work-table forms part of the contents of
Osterley Park and was perhaps used by
Mrs Child in her bedroom on the upper floor.

The top, decorated with a design of the
Firmament, is hinged to give access to the bag,
which has a wooden base.

T/10 WRITING-TABLE

Satinwood veneer, inlaid with various woods;
the interior covered with green baize; brass
handles; leather castors.
Late 18th century.
Height 84 cm. (33 in.).
Given by H. A. Bowler Esq.
W.40–1922.

The hinged top swings open to form trays,
which have baize-covered lids. A harlequin
fitment of 6 pigeon-holes above 3 shallow
drawers rises at the back when the release
mechanism is operated by means of a metal
catch under the table. In front of this fitment
there is a writing-flap that can be raised on a
ratchet, flanked by compartments with hinged
lids.

The top drawer is fitted with compartments of
various sizes, some of which have lids.

T/9

T/10

T/11   WRITING-CABINET ON STAND

Cedar, veneered with satinwood and root of walnut, and mahogany.
Late 18th century.
One of a pair.
Height 103 cm. (40½ in.).
290–1876.

The minute scale of this cabinet and the rather attenuated stand are typical of writing-furniture intended for the use of ladies at this time. The oval, used here to decorate the doors and sides, was a popular shape for inlaid, marquetry or painted decoration.

Inside there are pigeon-holes and drawers, one of the latter fitted with an ink-bottle and pounce pot. Below these there is a writing-slide of mahogany. The stand has a shallow drawer.

T/12   CORNER WASH-STAND

Beech, painted in various colours on a white ground.
About 1790.
Height (closed) 80 cm. (31½ in.).
W.29–1919.

This type of stand, having a double folding top, which, when opened, serves to protect the wall from splashes, is illustrated in *Sheraton*, pl. 42, where it is described as a 'Corner Bason Stand'. A wash-stand of similar design, which has splayed legs of this type, is illustrated in the records for 1793 of Gillow and Sons. This splaying of the legs is a feature sometimes introduced at this time and served to give greater stability to rather slender designs.

T/11

T/12

GROUP U

Commodes, large Cabinets, etc.

This section is devoted to larger items of
case-furniture and includes commodes,
dressing-tables and cabinets of various types.

The commode, U/5, is uncompromisingly
Neo-Classical in both form and ornament but
several of these pieces retain the serpentine
lines of the Rococo style; notably U/1, U/2 and
U/3.

U/1 COMMODE

Oak and pine, veneered with walnut, sycamore, fruitwood, purple-heart, tulipwood, kingwood and box; ormolu mounts.
About 1760.
Height 86.5 cm. (34 in.).
Bought with the aid of the National
Art-Collections Fund.
W.10–1957.

This commode has Neo-Classical details in the marquetry, although this is mainly, like the bombé shape, in the Rococo style. The decoration is very Germanic in appearance and has affinities with that on several commodes at Potsdam. However, the straight-sided back and the wooden (as opposed to marble) top point to its having been made in this country, a contention borne out by the appearance of the mounts. The likelihood of its having been made by an immigrant craftsman is supported by the roughness of the deal interior, as well as by the absence of dustboards between the drawers. There is a space between the drawers and the serpentine sides, and a small shelf, level with the base of each drawer, serving to give rigidity to the construction. The drawers, which are made of oak, are rabbetted at the bottom in the English way. The handles do not bear any relationship to the design and are probably later additions.

The commode was sold from Hagley Park, Worcestershire, in 1950 but it is not known whether it formed part of the original furnishings or was purchased to replace other furniture destroyed in the fire at Hagley on Christmas Eve, 1925.

U/1

U/2 COMMODE

Mahogany, inlaid with rosewood, satinwood, tulipwood, ebonized wood and stained woods; ormolu mounts.
About 1770.
Height 87.5 cm. (34½ in.).
W.30–1937.

This commode has a Rococo, bombé, shape but the decoration, incorporating the recently reintroduced floral marquetry, is of Neo-Classical type. The end panels have the straight edge at the back which is found on English, but not usually on Continental, commodes of this type.

The doors, hinged on the keel edges, enclose interior fittings consisting of three shelves above four short drawers. There are dustboards between the drawers and also panels, forming straight sides to the interior.

A number of related commodes have been recorded, one of them formerly in the collection of the Earl of Ilchester and another, formerly the property of the late Viscount Leverhulme and sold in New York in 1926. They are normally attributed to John Cobb owing to their close similarity to a very splendid commode supplied by him for Corsham Court, Wiltshire, in 1772.

U/2

U/3   COMMODE

Satinwood veneer, inlaid with laburnum, holly
and sycamore; gilt brass mounts.
About 1770.
Height 86 cm. (34 in.).
Given by Mrs H. H. Mulliner through
Freeman Smith Esq.
W.88–1924.

Like the preceding examples, this commode
has marquetry of Neo-Classical character
applied to a serpentine form. It is unusually
small for an English commode and is fitted
with one shelf inside.

Trophies of musical instruments, derived from
designs by Watteau, were much used during
the early years of the Neo-Classical movement
in France (G. de Bellaigue, 'English
Marquetry's Debt to France—II', *Country
Life*, vol. CXLIII, 20 June 1968, p. 1690).

U/3

U/4 COMMODE
Marquetry of harewood, purplewood and
mahogany.
About 1780.
Height 80.5cm. ($31\frac{3}{4}$in.).
Bequeathed by T. H. Loveless Esq.
W.10–1917.

This commode retains an irregular serpentine
plan but the decoration of fine quality
marquetry includes the usual Neo-Classical
motifs of paterae, ribbons, husks and antique
vases. The top has a large oval patera. The
feet are not original, having been made in 1961
to replace vase-shaped feet of nineteenth
century type.

A pair of commodes of similar design and
apparently from the same workshop, is in the
possession of Earl Mountbatten at Broadlands,
Hampshire.

U/4

U/5   COMMODE

Veneered with harewood and satinwood,
inlaid with tulipwood, burr walnut and holly.
1775/80.
Height 88.5 cm. (34¾ in.).
W.56–1925.

This commode is attributed to William Moore
of Dublin (W. A. Thorpe, 'William Moore,
Inlayer', *Country Life*, vol. XCIX, 3 May 1946,
p. 807, where it is compared to a similar one
bearing an ivory tab to the effect that 'It was
made by William Moore of Dublin for the
third Duke of Portland in 1782 when he was

Viceroy of Ireland'). It is also very similar to
one at Corsham Court, Wiltshire, the bill for
which is dated 1772.

Its simple, semi-circular plan is characteristic
of many commodes and side-tables designed at
this time and was a form greatly favoured by
Adam himself.

William Moore had been apprenticed to Ince
and Mayhew and it is interesting to note that
there is a distinct resemblance between the
marquetry on this piece and that on the
cabinet made for the Duchess of Manchester
by that firm in 1775 (N/4).

U/5

U/6 COMMODE

Satinwood, inlaid with rosewood and ivory and painted in various colours.
About 1790.
Height 86.5 cm. (34 in.).
636–1870.

This commode shows the translation into painted decoration of the recently revived floral marquetry.

The top is painted with a rustic scene within a central lunette, scrolling foliage and a border of peacock's feathers. The top drawer is fitted with a writing slide, let into which is a hinged flap, covered with blue velvet. There is a central well below, surrounded by compartments of various shapes and sizes, some of which have lids; two of these have removable linings of tin, which were perhaps intended to contain bottles of perfume, etc. Two other compartments are fitted with a clothes brush and a pin-cushion, respectively.

The keyholes have an ivory surround.

U/6

U/7   COMMODE

Satinwood, inlaid with mahogany and ivory
and painted in various colours.
One of a pair.
In the style of about 1790.
Height 89 cm. (35 in.).
Given by Mrs J. Garwood (Frank and Helen
Lloyd Bequest).
W.58a–1927.

The preceding commode, U/6, appears to have
been the model for this pair of commodes,
which may have been made shortly after the
first commode was acquired by the Museum in
1870.

The tops are decorated in the same way as that
of commode U/6 and the top drawer of each
has similar fittings for writing and dressing.

U/7

U/8   COMMODE

Pine, veneered with rosewood, satinwood and
other woods, some stained green; brass mounts.
Probably about 1785.
Height 89 cm. (35 in.).
H.H.30–1948.

This commode belongs to Ham House and may
perhaps be identifiable with the entry in the
inventory of 1844, which lists *A very curious
inlaid and gilt pier commode.*

The design, which is in the French Transitional
style, is apparently based on a commode signed
by P. A. Foullet, which appeared on the Paris
market in December, 1968. The front of the
Foullet commode is divided into two drawers,
without doors, in the normal French manner,
but the decorative details are almost identical,
except that some of the metal mounts have
been translated into marquetry decoration on
the Ham commode. The Foullet commode has
a top of white marble. (A secretaire in the

Wallace Collection, attributed to A. or P. A. Foullet (no. F.299), has a pair of oval mounts similar to those framing the central motif on each of the commodes.)

Several features of this commode point to an English origin. The carcase is of pine, which was usual in England, whereas the French used oak at this date for high-class furniture. The wooden top is also a feature found on English commodes but hardly ever on commodes made in France, where the practice was to have a marble slab. Finally, the use of two doors to mask the drawers or sliding trays was an English characteristic only very occasionally used on French commodes, in which case they were, in fact, referred to as being *à l'anglaise*.

U/8

The two doors extend across the full width of the front and there are two shallow drawers above them in the frieze. Inside there are two drawers, flanked on either side by a compartment with a shelf. The interior is smoothly finished in the English manner.

The use of marquetry sprays of flowers was revived in France in the mid-eighteenth century and quickly adopted in England. Trophies of musical instruments, derived from designs by Watteau, were much used during the early years of the Neo-Classical movement in France (G. de Bellaigue, 'English Marquetry's Debt to France—II', *Country Life*, vol. CXLIII, 20 June 1968, p. 1690).

U/9   DRESSING-COMMODE

Mahogany, inlaid with satinwood; the
mouldings ebonized.
About 1775.
Height 84cm. (33 in.).
Given by Eric M. Browett Esq.
W.55–1937.

The top drawer is fitted with an interior slide
covered with green baize, which gives access
to a central tilting and sliding mirror, flanked
by lidded compartments and trays, covering
recesses.

The bombé shape, which was introduced from
France shortly after the middle of the century,
has here been simplified. Only the upright

members flanking the front face of this
commode are shaped three-dimensionally. The
drawer-fronts are serpentine only in plan view
and the sides are practically straight. This
formula was much used in England from about
1765 onwards for all but the most elaborate
carcase-furniture. The splayed legs springing
from the serpentine skirting or apron are part
of the same formula. When commodes were of
rectilinear form or were serpentine in a
horizontal plane only, feet of the traditional
bracket type were normally used. The
survival of Rococo forms is seen also in the
asymmetrical back-plates of the handles, yet
the banding framing the drawer-fronts
reflects the return to popularity of inlay and

U/9

marquetry which became a feature of the
Neo-Classical movement, although the
inspiration sprang from French Rococo
furniture.

U/10   PEDESTAL DRESSING-TABLE

Mahogany, veneered with kingwood and
decorated with marquetry of various woods,
some stained green.
About 1775.
Height 79 cm. (31 in.).
Given through the National Art-Collections
Fund.
W.55–1928.

The top drawer is fitted with a central
adjustable hinged mirror, flanked by
compartments of various sizes and boxes for
toilet requisites. The pedestals each enclose
three drawers behind doors and there is a door
in the central recess, enclosing a cupboard with
a shelf. The unusual curved bracket feet
conceal large wooden castors, which may not be
original. The blocks under the feet appear to
have been added later to accommodate them.

U/10

U/11

U/11 DRESSING-TABLE

Satinwood, inlaid with various woods and
painted in various colours; grisaille medallions;
brass moulding surrounding the oval box;
engraved silver handles.
Probably about 1780 and restored in the
19th century.
Height 170 cm. (67 in.).
635–1870.

This piece has for some time been considered of
doubtful authenticity but it has, in fact, been in
the Museum since 1866, when it must already
have looked convincingly old, suggesting that
it is in the main an eighteenth-century piece,
in spite of its somewhat incongruous
appearance. Clearly it has been much restored
and possibly the whole superstructure is of later
date. The oval box on the delicately shaped
stretchers is also a strange feature. The dressing-
table was again restored in the early 1960s.

U/12

The acquisition of this piece by the South
Kensington Museum, which was established
expressly to provide inspiration for British
designers, may well have given impetus to the
vogue for furniture in the English late
eighteenth-century style that was so marked a
feature of the closing decades of the last
century (cf. the armchair by the nineteenth-
century firm of Wright and Mansfield, P/8).

A dressing-table in which a pivoted glass was
supported between two cabinets on the table
top had first been designed by Chippendale
(*Director*, 3rd ed., 1762, pl. LII). Hepplewhite
does not show any dressing-tables of this type in
the *Guide* but Sheraton illustrates a much more
complex version in the *Drawing Book* (pl. 49).

The frieze drawer of this dressing-table is
fitted with a baize-covered writing-slide, which
has recesses for writing-materials on either
side. In the middle there is a hinged book-rest,
which can be supported on ratchets.

A dressing-table made to the same design,
though with minor differences in the
execution, was exhibited at the Loan
Exhibition of English Furniture held at
Bethnal Green Museum in 1896.

U/12 CABINET ON STAND

Harewood veneer, with marquetry of various
woods, some stained green.
About 1775.
Height 133 cm. (52¼ in.).
W.2–1962.

The extremely attenuated cabriole legs are
characteristic of much furniture of this
period and quite different from the cabriole leg
of the early and mid-eighteenth century.
Curiously, the serpentine lines are restricted to
the stand, while the cabinet is completely
rectilinear. The marquetry of sprigs of flowers
is inspired by French work and resembles
that on the front of the commode at Ham
House, U/8.

U/13 SECRETAIRE-BOOKCASE

Satinwood, painted in various colours and
inlaid with different woods, some stained.
About 1785.
Height 183 cm. (72 in.).
Given by Sir Claude Phillips.
W.121–1924.

The hinged front of the top drawer lets down
on metal quadrants, released by press-buttons,
to form a writing-surface. *Hepplewhite*
illustrates two examples of a *Secretary and
Bookcase* with this feature, though neither is
of break-front type.

The unusual decoration round the top is
derived from acroteria or antefixes, motifs
from Classical architecture used by 'Athenian'
Stuart (on furniture made for Lady Spencer in
the 1760s) and by Adam (eg on the State Bed
at Osterley Park, H/1).

U/14 BUREAU-BOOKCASE

Satinwood, inlaid with rosewood; brass
handles.
Late 18th century.
Height 212.5 cm. (83¾ in.).
W.84–1910.

Enclosed behind the cylinder-front are
pigeon-holes, drawers and an adjustable
writing-leaf, covered with green leather.

The cylinder-front was a feature that probably
originated in Germany but is likely to have
reached this country via France. It was adopted
here towards the end of the eighteenth
century.

U/14

GROUP V

Firescreens and a Cheval Glass

This section contains a small group of
fire-screens of the pole and cheval type,
together with a cheval glass. The terms,
'horse-screen', or 'horse-glass', were also
used in the eighteenth century.

V/1   POLE-SCREEN
Mahogany; panel of painted silk, attached with brass rings.
About 1775.
Height 123 cm. (48½ in.).
O.P.H.326–1949.

This pole-screen forms part of the furnishings of Osterley Park. The painted silk is similar to that used for the furniture from the Taffeta Bedroom (see Group L), suggesting that this screen may have been used in that room, although the rest of the furniture is of satinwood.

The slender cabriole legs, of the type sometimes used in the second half of the eighteenth century, are similar to those of the reading stand, S/12. One of the three pole-screens illustrated in *Hepplewhite*, 1st ed., 1788, has legs of cabriole type (pl. 93).

V/1

V/2

V/2 POLE-SCREEN
Painted black with decoration in various
colours; glazed panel containing an
embroidered picture.
One of a pair.
About 1785.
Height 157.5 cm. (62 in.).
W.15–1951.

In this pole-screen, the shield shape, so
popular for the backs of chairs, has been used
for the panel. No illustrations of a pole-screen
with such a panel appear in *Hepplewhite*,
but *Sheraton* shows one screen which has a
shield-shaped panel (pl. 38), although the
design as a whole is much more complex.

V/3   POLE-SCREEN
Satinwood, with painted decoration in various
colours; the panel painted in various colours on
a buff ground.
About 1785.
Height 145 cm. (57 in.).
W.51–1950.

Hepplewhite illustrates a pole-screen with an
oval panel in the *Guide*, 1st ed., 1788, pl. 93,
but this has a solid base. The type of tripod
seen in this example, sometimes called a
'claw', was commonly adopted towards the
end of the century.

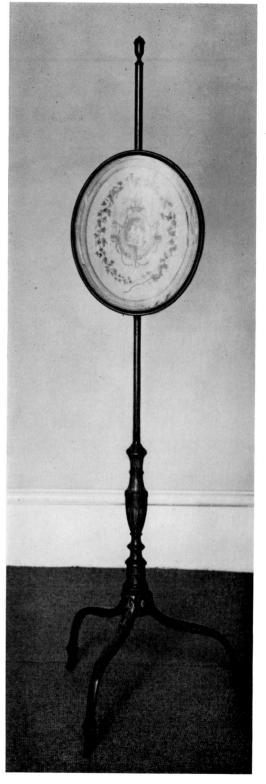

V/3

V/4

V/4   CHEVAL FIRE-SCREEN
Mahogany with a tapestry panel.
Of uncertain date.
Height 139 cm. (54¾ in.).
Bequeathed by Claude Rotch Esq.
W.56–1962.

This screen, which is embellished with the
popular Neo-Classical motifs of the Prince of
Wales's feathers at the top and a ribbon bow at
the base of the panel, was probably made
within the last fifty years to hold the tapestry
panel.

The tapestry, which is on a burgundy-red
ground, is signed *Nielson. ex*. Jacques Nielson
was in charge of a tapestry-weaving atelier at
the Gobelins works between 1749 and 1788.
He wove a number of designs after Boucher,
including those for the Tapestry Room at
Osterley Park (Group G). Imitations of
tapestries in this style, sometimes signed, are
not unknown, however. This panel, which is
worn, is backed with a nineteenth-century
silk-and-cotton material.

V/5

V/5   CHEVAL GLASS
Satinwood, painted in various colours and
inlaid with ebony stringing lines; brass
mounts.
About 1790.
Height 168 cm. (66 in.).
Given by Eric M. Browett Esq. in memory of
his wife, Ada Mary Browett.
W.58–1937.

The floral ornament is painted in naturalistic
colours but the cupids in the oval at the base
are *en grisaille*. The stand is also painted on
the back; at the top there is scrolling foliage
surrounding a cupid within an oval medallion
and at the bottom a trophy of musical
instruments.

There is a glass of rather similar design
illustrated in *Sheraton*, 3rd ed., 1802, pl. XVII.

The splayed legs, terminating in brass caps, to
which the castors are fixed, are of a type that
was widely used at this time, particularly for
tables.

GROUP W

Urns and Pedestals

This group contains urns and pedestals, items
which formed part of the furnishing of a
dining room. Adam frequently flanked his
sideboards with a pair of urns standing on
pedestals, to form an imposing array at one end
of the room (C/3 and C/4). This formula was
widely adopted by other designers. Later the
urns came to be placed actually on the
sideboard itself, which was then provided with
drawers. The urns were sometimes fitted with
compartments for cutlery; others were lined
with lead to hold water which, through a tap
in the lower front of the urn, could be poured
into a lined tray-like drawer behind concealed
doors in the front of the pedestal. A butler
could rinse cutlery or glasses in these small
basins. Yet other pedestals were lined with
sheet-iron and provided with racks and a small
brazier, so that plates could be kept warm in
them.

W/1   KNIFE-CASE
Marquetry of various coloured woods; velvet
lining.
One of a pair.
Late 18th century.
Height 47.5 cm. (18¾ in.).
352–1870.

The top can be raised on a central shaft, around
which compartments for cutlery are arranged
concentrically.

W/2   URN
Mahogany; lined with red velvet.
One of a pair.
About 1790.
Height 67.5 cm. (26½ in.).
Bequeathed by Dr T. R. C. Whipham through
Barclays Bank Ltd.
W.8–1945.

There are signs that the velvet lining was put
in later to cover unevenness in the wood when
a fitting was removed. This suggests that these
urns, which are now hollow, were originally
fitted up as knife-cases. This somewhat raw
appearance indicates that for some reason the
old polish was entirely removed.

W/1

W/2

W/3 KNIFE-BOX
Mahogany, inlaid with satinwood.
One of a pair.
About 1800.
Height 73.5 cm. (29 in.).
Given by Miss Errington Loveland and
R. Errington Loveland Esq.
W.35–1947.

W/4 URN
Painted satinwood.
About 1790.
Height 73.5 cm. (29 in.).
W.67–1925.

The inside is covered with paper.

W/3

W/4

W/5 PEDESTAL CUPBOARD

Mahogany, with brass mounts.
About 1760.
Height 94 cm. (37 in.).
Bequeathed by Claude Rotch Esq.
W.39–1962.

This piece, which must have been designed to
accompany a sideboard, may be compared with
the pedestals, A/5, of which it is a simpler
version, without the urns.

The top can be extended by means of two
flaps, supported on brass-handled lopers.
There is a door in the front, with a drawer
below. The cupboard has a shelf and is pierced
at the back with circular air-holes.

W/6 PEDESTAL

Mahogany, inlaid with various woods; brass
mounts; Wedgwood plaque with a white
figure on a black ground.
One of a pair.
Of uncertain date.
Height 113.5 cm. (44¾ in.).
398–1874.

This curious piece incorporates sections of high
quality but the back appears to have been
extended, while the skirting and moulding
round the top are probably also additions. What
the original purpose of this piece may have
been is not clear. However, the decoration is of
an Adamesque form while the recessed
colonnettes seem to owe something to French
furniture of the late eighteenth century.

W/5

W/6

GROUP X

Clocks

Clocks showing Neo-Classical characteristics are
contained in this section. The form of long-case
clocks remained static throughout the
Neo-Classical period; even Neo-Classical
decorative features are often limited to the
smallest details (X/1). Bracket clocks were often
equally conservative, although the innovatory
'balloon' form (X/3) first appeared at this time.

X/1

X/1   LONG-CASE CLOCK
Oak, veneered with walnut; brass mounts.
About 1780.
Height 239 cm. (94 in.).
Bequeathed by Mrs Gertrude M. Winstanley.
W.21–1946.

Engraved *Frans Jullion London* on a plate on
the face.

The two keyhole escutcheons are the only
overtly Neo-Classical features on this clock.

X/2

X/2 LONG-CASE CLOCK

Mahogany case, inlaid with satinwood; painted
decoration on hood and face; brass mounts.
North American; about 1785.
Height 249 cm. (98 in.).
W.13–1955.

Painted in black on the dial *Mitchell & Mott /
New York*. Henry Mitchell was made a
freeman of New York in 1787; Mott was
recorded as having been in partnership with a
certain Morne in New York in 1805.

Inside the door is pasted a piece of paper with
the written inscription *This clock was brought
to Fort Neck, South Oyster Bay, (now
Massapequa, Nassau County) Long Island,
State of New York, by Sarah Onderdonk, the
bride of David Richard Floyd, in 1785*.

This clock is of an English type and is included
here for convenience, since the Museum's
collection of American furniture is very small.

X/3   BRACKET CLOCK
The case veneered with satinwood, cross-
banded with tulipwood; brass feet.
About 1790.
Height 41.9 cm. (16½ in.).
Bequeathed by Arthur Penrose Milstead Esq.
W.18–1951.

Inscribed on the face *Perigal and Browne
London*. This firm of clockmakers was active in
Coventry Street between 1782 and 1799.

This type of spring-driven clock, having a
waisted case, was known as a 'balloon clock'.
The oval decorative feature contains a
representation of the Prince of Wales's
feathers.

X/3

GROUP Y

Musical Instruments

This section is devoted to musical instruments of the keyboard type, decorated under the influence of the Neo-Classical movement. Detailed descriptions of these instruments, with full technical information, may be found in R. Russell, *Catalogue of Musical Instruments*, Victoria and Albert Museum, vol. I, *Keyboard Instruments*, London, 1968, in which there is a section on the *Decoration of Keyboard Instruments* by Peter Thornton (pp. 71–5).

Musical instruments are of particular interest to the furniture historian because they often bear a date and provenance. However, English keyboard instruments of the eighteenth century continued to have cases veneered with walnut long after mahogany had come into general use in this country. This was presumably due to a preference among the makers of cases for such instruments, whose trade was a specialized one, like that of the makers of clock cases.

Y/1   SQUARE PIANOFORTE
Mahogany, inlaid with holly stringing.
Dated 1767.
Height 16.5 cm. (6½ in.).
W.27–1928.

The inscription behind the keyboard reads
Johannes Zumpe Londini Fecit 1767. This is
one of the earliest English pianofortes, the
first recorded instrument being dated 1766.

The stand is separate from the instrument, as it
is in the early clavichord form, from which the
square pianoforte is derived.

Russell, cat. no. 29.

Y/1

Y/2   SQUARE PIANOFORTE
Mahogany, inlaid with holly stringing; the mahogany base has brass castors.
Dated 1773.
Height 80 cm. (31½ in.).
O.P.H.158–1949.

This piano, which forms part of the contents of Osterley Park, is inscribed *Johannes Pohlman Londini Fecit 1773*.

Pohlman (sometimes spelt Pohlmann) was probably one of the twelve followers of Zumpe who fled to this country from Germany at the time of the Seven Years War. He worked in London between 1767 and 1793, producing square pianofortes on the Zumpe model at his premises in Compton Street, Soho, and 113 Great Russell Street, where he achieved a success nearly as great as that of his master (cf. the pianoforte by Zumpe, Y/1).

This instrument is a good example of the earliest phase of piano building in England, in a fine state of preservation. The keys are faced with ebony, the sharps being of pearwood stained black and capped with a slip of ivory; the black keyboard is a most unusual feature for an English instrument of this period.

When restoration was being carried out in 1969 the discovery was made, beneath the keyboard, of a number of invitation cards to *Mr. Arnold Dolmetsch's Series of Three Concerts at 7, Bayley Street, Bedford Square, on Wednesday evening July 12th, 19th and 26th, 1899 at 8.30 o'clock*.

There is no mention of this instrument in the inventory of the contents of Osterley Park, made in 1782. It is not recorded in the Museum's Catalogue of Musical Instruments except in a note among the Addenda.

I am indebted to Mr Derek Adlam for information about this pianoforte.

Y/2

Y/3   HARPSICHORD

Mahogany veneer, inlaid with harewood
stringing; the keyboard surround veneered
with panels of burr walnut, cross-banded with
tulipwood and inlaid with harewood stringing.
Dated 1776.
Height 32 cm. (12½ in.).
Given by F. S. Dayman Esq.
W.43–1927.

The harpsichord is inscribed above the
keyboards *Jacobus et Abraham Kirckman
fecerunt 1776.*

It has an adjustable music desk, an unusual
feature in an eighteenth-century harpsichord
made in London.

Russell, cat. no. 25.

Y/3

Y/4   HARPSICHORD

Mahogany veneer, cross-banded with
satinwood and inlaid with harewood.
Dated 1782.
Height 32.5 cm. (12¾ in.).
Given by Charles Hey Laycock Esq.
W.13–1943.

The harpsichord is inscribed above the
keyboards *Burkat Shudi et Johannes Broadwood
No. 919, 1782.*

Like the Kirckman harpsichord (Y/3), it is
fitted with an adjustable music desk.

Russell, cat. no. 26.

Y/5   CHAMBER ORGAN

Mahogany, inlaid with various woods.
Dated 1786.
Height 526 cm. (207 in.).
303–1900.

The case is inscribed above the keyboard
Daniel Prior Londini Fecit 1786.

The present front, decorated with a large oval
having a patera in the centre, is a later
alteration, presumably made to replace dummy
pipes, which were often used on such cases.

Russell, cat. no. 47.

Y/4

Y/5

BIBLIOGRAPHY

ADAM, R., and J. *The Works in Architecture.* 2 vols. London, 1773–79; third volume, 1822 (Reprints: Thezard, 1902; Tiranti, 1939 and 1959).

BOLTON, A. T. *The Architecture of Robert and James Adam.* 2 vols. London, 1922.

Connoisseur Period Guides, The. *Late Georgian: 1760–1810.* London, 1961.

EDWARDS, R., *ed. Dictionary of English Furniture.* 3 vols. 2nd ed. London, 1954.

EDWARDS, R., and JOURDAIN, M. *Georgian Cabinet-Makers.* 3rd ed. London, 1955.

EDWARDS, R., WATSON, F. J. B., and HARRIS, J. 'Neo-Classic Furniture: The Battle of the Styles' (correspondence), *Apollo*, vol. LXXXVII, February 1968, p. 66. (Reply by P. K. Thornton, *Apollo*, vol. LXXXVII, April 1968, p. 310.)

ERIKSEN, S. 'Lalive de Jully's Furniture "à la grècque"', *Burlington Magazine*, vol. CIII, August 1961, p. 340.

ERIKSEN, S. 'Marigny and "Le Goût Grec"', *Burlington Magazine*, vol. CIV, March 1962, p. 96.

ERIKSEN, S. 'Early Neo-Classicism in French Furniture', *Apollo*, vol. LXXVIII, November 1963.

FASTNEDGE, R. *English Furniture Styles from 1500 to 1830.* London, 1955.

FASTNEDGE, R. *Shearer Furniture Designs.* London, 1962.

FASTNEDGE, R. *Sheraton Furniture.* London, 1962.

FLEMING, J. *Robert Adam and his Circle.* London, 1962.

HARRIS, E. 'Robert Adam and the Gobelins', *Apollo*, April 1962.

HARRIS, E. *The Furniture of Robert Adam.* London, 1963.

HARRIS, J. 'Early Neo-Classical Furniture', *Furniture History*, *The Journal of the Furniture History Society*, vol. II, 1966, p. 1.

HARRIS, J. 'Le Gueay, Piranesi and International Neo-Classicism in Rome 1740–1750', *Essays in the History of Architecture presented to Rudolf Wittkower.* London, 1967.

HARRIS, J. *Sir William Chambers.* London, 1970.

HAYWARD, H. 'The Drawings of John Linnell in the Victoria and Albert Museum', *Furniture History*, *The Journal of the Furniture History Society*, vol. V, 1969, p. 1.

HEAL, SIR A. *The London Furniture Makers from the Restoration to the Victorian Era 1660–1840.* London, 1953.

HEPPLEWHITE, A. and Co. *The Cabinet-Maker and Upholsterer's Guide.* 1st ed. London, 1788; 2nd ed. 1789; 3rd ed. 1794.

HONOUR, H. *Neo-Classicism.* London, 1968.

JOURDAIN, M. *English Decoration and Furniture of the Late XVIII Century.* London, 1922.

JOURDAIN, M. *English Interiors in Smaller Houses.* London, 1923.

KIMBALL, F. 'Les Influences anglaises dans la Formation du Style Louis XVI', *Gazette des Beaux-Arts*, 6th ser., vol. V, 1951, p. 29.

KIMBALL, F. 'The Moor Park Tapestry Suite of Furniture by Robert Adam', *Philadelphia Museum Bulletin*, vol. XXXVI, no. 189, March 1941, p. 35.

KIMBALL, F. *The Creation of the Rococo.* Philadelphia, 1943.

LEES-MILNE, J. *The Age of Adam.* London, 1947.

MUSGRAVE, C. *Adam and Hepplewhite and other Neo-Classical Furniture.* London, 1966.

NEUFFORGE, J.-F. de. *Recueil d'Architecture.* 10 vols. Paris, 1757–77.

SHEARER, T. *The Cabinet-Maker's London Book of Prices.* London, 1788.

SHERATON, T. *The Cabinet-Maker and Upholsterer's Drawing Book.* London, 1791–94.

STILLMAN, D. *The Decorative Work of Robert Adam.* London, 1966.

SUMMERSON, SIR J. *Architecture in Britain 1530–1830.* 3rd ed. London, 1958.

SWARBRICK, J. *Robert Adam and his Brothers.* London, 1916.

SWARBRICK, J. *The Works in Architecture of Robert and James Adam.* London, 1959.

SYMONDS, R. W. 'Adam and Chippendale: A Myth Exploded', *Country Life Annual*, 1958, p. 53.

THORNTON, P. K., and HARDY, J. 'The Spencer Furniture at Althorp' (Sections II and III, dealing with furniture by 'Athenian' Stuart), *Apollo*, vol. LXXXVII, June 1968, p. 440 and vol. LXXXVIII, October 1968, p. 266.

VICTORIA AND ALBERT MUSEUM. RUSSELL R. *Catalogue of Musical Instruments*, vol. I, *Keyboard Instruments.* London, 1968.

VICTORIA AND ALBERT MUSEUM. TOMLIN, M. F. *Osterley Park.* London, 1972.

VICTORIA AND ALBERT MUSEUM. WARD-JACKSON, P. W. *English Furniture Designs of the Eighteenth Century.* London, 1958.

WATSON, F. J. B. *Louis XVI Furniture.* London, 1961.

INDEX